Island Walks

Dieter Graf

Walking on Naxos

GW00536284

Hiking and Swimming for Island-Hoppers
25 Walks with GPS data

Graf Editions

Using this illustrated walking guide

AWT stands for Actual Walking Time. This time does not include breaks, wrong turns or sight-seeing. The AWT serves as a personal control as to whether certain route markings, emphasized in **bold print**, have been reached in the given time. These times are an aid for orientation and should not be considered as encouragement to achieve a record performance. Spot heights are added in brackets.

The approximate **overall length** of a walk is specified in hours in the introduction to each tour. These figures do not include time taken for bus trips or extra-long breaks. Information concerning the **length of the walks**, the **difference in altitude** and three **levels of difficulty** can also be found there. **Spot heights** are added in brackets.

Route photos are intended for orientation, for consulting locals and as a stimulus. The corresponding text is marked by ⊡ to ④. The **route sketches** have been drawn to the best of our knowledge but lay no claim to completeness.

GPS points are shown as P in texts and on maps. Map datum WGS84. The GPS data can be downloaded from the publisher's website.

We would be grateful for information concerning **changes** in paths and similar data. As a token of our appreciation we will send you a free copy of our next edition.

The website www.graf-editions.de informs you of any changes that occur along walking routes.

The author Dieter Graf is an architect who has travelled all over the world. He has walked the Aegean Islands since the years when tourism was just beginning there and is considered a connoisseur of the islands. For this book he spent many months on the Dodecanese Islands.

© 2011 Edition Dieter Graf, Elisabethstr. 29, 80796 München
        Tel. 0049-(0)89-271 59 57, Fax 0049-(0)89-271 59 97
        www.graf-editions.de

Type-Setting: Michael Henn, Ottobrunn · Maps: Kurt Zucher, Wielenbach
Original Title: »Wandern auf Naxos« (ISBN 978-3-9808802-8-2)

Cover Photo: Ayios Geórgios o Diassorítis ⑦

ISBN 978-3-9808802-9-9

Contents

Náxos

Already when you sail into the harbour, you can sense the island's tremendous cultural diversity. On the left, you peer up at the enormous portal of a classical temple; on the right, you glide past a small Byzantine chapel and, towering above the huddled Cycladic city, a Venetian kástro from the Middle Ages. The city, dating back 5000 years, is one of the oldest inhabited places in the world.

When you penetrate further in to the island, you are surprised by the diversity of the fertile landscapes. An enormous rugged mountain massif – consisting of granite, gneiss and marble with three peaks rising to an altitude of almost 1000 metres – forms the background for the green heart of the island, the Tragéa plain, covered with olive groves and ancient oaks. Stretching further to the west is extensive farming land, until it meets a never-ending landscape of dunes along the seaside. Connoisseurs of small bathing bays can find wonderful spots along the rocky east coast.

However, it is not just nature which surprises with its enormous abundance. People have also left outstanding buildings during their long habitation of the island. Except in the lively Mediterranean harbour city, they tended – for reasons of security – to live in compact mountain villages which allow us, even today, to trace the tracks of old Greece. In addition to the whitewashed cube houses, there are also a great number of castle-like residences from the Venetian nobility of the Middle Ages as well as fortress-like Orthodox and even Catholic monasteries. Art-lovers find not only the remains of classical temple complexes, but also monumental statues worked on by artists and left behind in ancient quarries. The Byzantine chapels from a later period house Early Medieval frescoes. Many finds from the numerous excavations on Náxos can be admired in the local museums. For many visitors Náxos is the most beautiful island of the Cyclades, not least because it has been spared mass tourism. The pleasantly relaxed hospitality extended here will remain in the memory for a long while. Even the gods of the Greek Pantheon felt extremely comfortable here.

Have a good trip. *Kaló taxídi*!

Walking on Naxos

Thanks to its varied landscape and lush vegetation, which distinguishes it from most of the other, more barren Cyclades, Náxos is one of the finest hiking islands in Greece. Moreover, the hiker still finds many intact **old mule tracks.** For centuries these narrow *monopátia* used to help the farmers work the fields and, up until 30 years ago, formed a dense network of tracks (see p. 26 ④).

By contrast, the up to four metre wide paved tracks, the *kalderímia,* connected larger villages for the transport of goods and served as paths for pilgrims to the monasteries. They were paved with marble and bordered with walls. Some of them are said to be up to 1000 years old (see p. 81 ④).

Motorisation has not failed to leave its mark on the islands either. Instead of mules the farmers now use pickups, which require wider roadways. The old network of tracks was torn apart by broadening the mule tracks to make them accessible to cars wherever it seemed to be necessary and by pushing aside the characteristic dry walls along the waysides, all co-financed by money from the European Union Regional Funds. The remaining paths are now superfluous and in ruins and are gradually being forgotten by the islanders. Lately, however, the EU Leader Fund provides money to restore some of the remaining mule tracks, mainly for the sake of tourism. Instead of maintaining and extending the scope of the network, however, this often only amounts to the over-perfect restoration of individual paths. This book aims to help ensure that the old mule tracks which still exist are used again and hence preserved before they are irreparably destroyed. They may, above all in spring, be rather overgrown!

The routes described have been walked along again shortly before publication and can be followed without difficulty by people in normal physical condition. Some of the walks are suitable for children. Special surefootedness is not necessary. The ✓ markings in the text concern only those who are very afraid of heights. For longer walking tours short cuts are indicated. Due to the good views, the tours normally lead from the mountains to the sea – so take along your swimming gear. You should be absolutely sure to pick a nice day for tours in the mountains since there is always the danger of sudden fog formation. Moreover it can rain there even in summer. On the other hand there is a risk of bush fires in the summer.

If you want to walk alone, you should by all means leave information in your hotel and save the number of the hotel on your mobile phone. In order to get your blood circulation going, you should begin leisurely for the first fifteen minutes and, during the tour, eat and especially drink often, even if you don't feel the need to do so. The route maps show springs and wells to be found by the wayside. Be sure to protect yourself sufficiently against sun and wind too.

Coloured dots and arrows can often be found as **markings along paths**, but they do not necessarily correspond to the descriptions in this book. In addition there are the wooden signs and little red-and-white metal signs of the Greek organisations. In 2008 a marked long-distance hiking trail was opened from Náxos town right across the island to Apóllonas (www.naxos.gr >Hiking, see p. 28). A good 1:40,000 **hiking map** from the Greek Anavási publishers is available in various shops.

As new roadways continue to be built, it may be that the route descriptions are partly out of date, thus calling for certain **orientation skills.** If you have orientation problems, you should always ask the locals about the "monopáti", otherwise you will be directed to roads for vehicular traffic. Mule dung on the narrow paths is more certain to lead you further than goat droppings since the goat paths usually end somewhere in the scrub, while mules always return to their stalls. If you lose your way, you may have to shin up a field wall or climb over steel mesh used as grazing fences with the help of a pile of stones. Pasture fences are knotted shut on the side where there are two perpendicular rods. You owe it to the farmers whose land you walk across to shut the openings again afterwards, of course. Access to the sea is allowed in Greece as a matter of principle.

Almost all the starting and finishing points are served by **public buses**, even in the low season. In case a service does not operate on Sundays, take a taxi. You should always make a point of settling the price before you begin the trip. The taximeter is only turned on when you specifically request it. A possibility for circular walking tours is a relatively reasonable rental car or a rental motor bike. In addition, car drivers also enjoy taking along a wanderer who waves him down.

Walks which are particularly recommended:
② ④ ⑨ ⑩ ⑪ ⑭ ⑯ ⑱ ㉑ ㉔

Appropriate hiking gear includes a backpack for a day, shoes with good soles (no sandals), comfortable socks, long trousers or zipper trousers*, possibly a mobile phone, binoculars, a whistle, a small flashlight and picnic equipment (with salt-shaker). In the spring and autumn, rainwear is a necessity. A compass would also be good, but is not necessary if you have a fairly good sense of orientation.

*The legs of zipper trousers which also have vertical zippers can be zipped together to form a pad to sit on at the beach. And if you connect both zippers, you have a chic skirt for visiting monasteries.

Climate and Walking Seasons

The climate on Náxos corresponds to that on the other Cyclades with a hot and dry summer and a mild rainy winter. The maximum **air temperature** is 32 °C in August (at night 22 °C). In the walking months May/June and September temperatures range between 19° and 24°. In winter the temperature sinks to 15 °C (7 °C) in February. On mountains above 800 m snow can fall and lie for a short while.

The **water temperatures** vary between 16 °C in February and almost 25 °C in August. You can go swimming from the end of May at 19 °C through to October (22 °C).

The rainy days are spread irregularly throughout the year. Most of the rain falls in December and January, when it rains on about 14 days. You must still calculate with 3 days of rain in May, while there is absolute dryness from June to August. Statistically September has 2 and October 6 days of rain, but it is not very plentiful.

The number of **hours of sunshine** per day corresponds to this pattern. In December and January the very strong winter sun only shines for about 4½ hours. Even in May the wanderer must reconcile himself to 10 hours of sunshine per day and the swimmer to 12 in August. October is once again pleasant for autumn walkers, with 7¾ hours of sunshine per day.

The Cyclades mainly have strong **north winds**, although Náxos is somewhat protected from these by having Mýkonos off the north coast. One reason for this is the difference in air pressure between the Azore highs and the hot low pressure areas above the Persian Gulf. In the transition season, especially in April and May and then October and November, the Boréas dominates, a cool, wet north wind. In the summer (May to September) the famous etesien winds, called the *meltémia*, blow up to force five or six and normally abate towards evening. All the same, the sea remains relatively calm and the sky clear but misty. The *sirocco* occurs less frequently, but especially in spring. It comes from the hot Sahara desert, picking up moisture over the Mediterranean to bring the Aegean warm humidity.

On the Greek islands there are several different **seasons for walking** tours. Anyone wishing to feast his eyes should plan his tour around Easter. It might be somewhat cool and even muddy, but the countryside is grass-green, poppy-red and broom-yellow; the houses and alleyways are freshly whitewashed. The preparations for the Greek Easter celebration alone make the trip worthwhile. However, you can't go swimming yet, and some hotels and tavernas are still closed. In April it can rain briefly. The Greeks divide the year into three parts, and this one is called "the time of blossoming and maturing".

In May and June the blossom time is already partially over, but, since it is very warm and the number of tourists is still limited, this is probably the most attractive time for walking. Beginning at the end of May the water has a pleasant temperature.

The main tourist season in July and August is not highly recommended for walking tours due to the heat. It is the "dry period" in Greece. The dry north winds, which blow continuously, still make the temperatures bearable, but at noon it is wise to seek a shady spot under a tree. Harvest time begins in July. On 15th August, the Assumption of the Virgin, called "Passing Away Peacefully" in the Eastern Church, there are great celebrations everywhere with roast lamb, music and dance.

From the beginning of September on, the heat is over and the sea still has a pleasant temperature for swimming, up until the end of October. Now it is again possible to take longer walking tours, but only until about 6 pm due to the shorter period of daylight. The land has become yellow and brown, the fields bear their fruit, and everywhere you meet friendly farmers harvesting their last crops. From the beginning of October on, it can start to rain again. The restaurants and hotels gradually shut down and some owners travel to their winter residences in Athens. Others put on camouflage suits, reach for their guns and search through the undergrowth. A million Greeks are passionate hunters. In November there is usually a change in climate, with heavy rainfall. Then it becomes unpleasant. The period from November to February is called the "rain season". Although there are some warm, sunny days around Christmas, it is more pleasant at home.

Geology

The Aegean Sea was not flooded by the sea until after the last ice age. Up until then the present island arc between Crete and Rhodes formed the southern edge of the mainland.

The more northern Cycladic islands stand on a submarine mountain which was raised out of the sea 50 million years ago by the pressure of the African continental plate on the European continental plate. After repeated rising and subsiding the islands assumed their current form. That is why one encounters slate, a sedimentary rock which was lifted out of the sea and sits on top of a bed of marble and granite. Náxos is especially rich in marble, although this does not reach the quality of that found on Páros. Embedded inside this is auburn emery, an extremely hard and heavy conglomerate consisting of magnetic iron ore, mica and corundum. The emery in the north of Náxos is the best natural emery in the world (see p. 102).

On the southern edge of the Aegean an active seismic arc extends from the Peleponnesus via the islands Póros, Mílos, Santoríni, Anáfi, Níssiros and Kos as far as the Taurus mountain range in Turkey. The pressure created by the land masses discharges itself here now and again as earthquakes. Half the earthquakes in Europe occur in Greece. Náxos, however, is seismically quieter.

Fauna

In contrast to the flora the variety of the animal kingdom is limited. As a result of the mostly low vegetation large game is not encountered. Hares and martens are seldom. The animals one most often comes across are goats and sheep, though not in such large numbers as in former years. Sometimes even pasture land is burned off, in order to create fresh nutriments for goats. The few cows have an almost exotic charm.

Of the smaller animals one hears and sees the small common lizard, which can be up to 10 cm long. The dragon-like agama (hardun) ①, its bigger relative, is up to 30 cm long. Even land turtles have now become rare.

The careful wanderer will rarely see snakes. There is only one poisonous type: the horn or sand viper ②. It can be up to 50 cm long and as thick as two thumbs. A healthy adult hardly need fear a deadly bite.

The non-poisonous sand-boa is about the same size. The non-poisonous four-striped-adder reaches an adult length of more

than a metre and a width almost as thick as an arm. Its size is frightening, but it is harmless, as is the ring-snake. As long as one does not move completely silently, the snakes disappear again. Long trousers give additional protection. On no account should one lift up large stones, as snakes may be sleeping underneath them.

The up to 5 cm long scorpions also hide there. The bite of a scorpion is rather painful but not deadly. They also love to hide in shoes.

You can rouse crabs, frogs and eels along the watercourses. In rocky bays you should look out for sea urchins ③.

Soaring above in search of prey are birds such as buzzards, falcons and griffon vultures; unfortunately migratory birds often fall victim to the Greek passion for hunting.

Flora

Ever since antiquity forests on the Aegean islands have been cut down for building ships or have fallen victim to forest fires in

summer, causing some parts of the countryside to seem like karstland. This effect is intensified by the limestone soil which cannot store water. Nevertheless, along with Spain, Greece has the greatest variety of plants in Europe. While there may be no forest hikes, it is still possible to find shady trails in the Pláka between the tall windbreaks made of reeds ①.

The **stock of trees** consists mainly of solitary specimens. Taller evergreen oaks and kermes oaks ② grow in protected regions which are rich in water. Unassuming, salt-tolerant tamarisks ③ are found along beaches. Plane-trees ④ shade the village squares and slender cypresses the cemeteries. Acacias, poplars, alders, maples and eucalyptus trees ⑤ can also be found, as well as mulberry trees ⑥ and carobs ⑦. Among the fruit trees there are pomegranates, fig trees ⑧ and citrus fruits. Yet dominating the landscape most of all is the olive tree, which looks strangely deformed as it gets older.

In the open countryside dry shrubs reaching a height of up to half a metre predominate, thorny undergrowth (garrigue) called **phrýgana** in Greek. Typical representatives of this "low mac-

chia" are broom, thorny knap-weed, heather, spiny spurge plants (euphorbia) 9 10, plants often shaped like hedgehogs. Jerusalem sage, squill and asphodel 11 blossom there.

Thicker bush or tree groups up to two metres high with evergreens and bushes with hard leaves are not found as frequently. This "high macchia" is called **xerovoúmi** in Greek. Kermes oaks with serrated leaves 2, juniper and mastic bushes 12 are particularly predominant. Mastic bushes are used for manufacturing rubber and raki spirits.

The agave 13, attributed to the cactus family, often lines the lanes and paths. This thorny leaf plant has only grown in the Mediterranean area since the 16th century. The fruit of the fig-cactus 14 makes a sweet supplement to any hiker's picnic.

Flowers can mainly be appreciated in spring. Already in January the anemone and crocus blossom. Then, from February through to May/June, all the splendour of white and red blossoming rockroses 15, iris, yellow daffodils, hyacinths, lupines, chrysanthemums and broom add magic to the landscape with their cheery colours, and the poppy adds its bright red.

Small orchids are an adornment of spring for a short time. The bee orchid (ophrys) 16, lax-flowered orchid (orchis), tongue orchid (serapias) and dragon arum 17 can be seen frequently.

In May and June the main blossoming season comes to an end, but summer doesn't mean brown wilderness by any means. Bougainvillea radiates its bright colours on the house walls, and oleander blossoms in moist spots. The thorny acanthus 18 and the gold thistle 19 bloom along the wayside.

When the summer heat subsides, meadow-saffron, heather and squill reveal themselves along with the dandelions, thistles and cyclamen.

Sage 20, capers 21 and other kitchen herbs often border the walking paths. While walking you can especially appreciate the pleasantly spicy aroma of thyme, rosemary, lavender, oregano, camomile and fennel.

Cultivated in the coastal plains are potatoes, wheat and vegetables and, on the Tragéa plateau, olives.

A brief history

The Cyclades have been settled since the Mesolithic period (7500 BC). Traces of settlements dating back to the end of the 4th millennium BC have been proven on Kéa and near Páros. The islands' position between Europe and Asia makes them a bridge between the two cultures and one of the oldest landscapes in Europe to be cultivated very early. During the transition from the Stone Age to the Bronze Age Europe experiences its first artistic climax, the Cycladic culture (3200–1100 BC). The seemingly modern flat female figures made of marble are famous. The most important finds have been made on Náxos (Grótta, Lóuros and Spedós), on Sýros and the now uninhabited Kéros.

Four thousand years ago the Phoenicians arrive from the coast of what is now Lebanon. They impart the skills of the Assyrians and Babylonians to the Greeks, as well as introducing writing and money. They are interested in trade rather than colonization. Then the islands come under the influence of Minoan Crete. Following the decline of the Cretan palaces around 1450 BC Mycenaean settlers from the Peleponnesus land and dictate subsequent events. On the mainland the Indo-European Dorians immigrating from the north later trigger a migration of peoples. After 1100 BC the islands of the Aegean and Asia Minor are colonized from there in several waves. The northern Cyclades are dominated by the Ionians.

Archaic Period　(800–500 BC) The Ionians are the first to release the Greek spirit in the sense of artistic, intellectual and economic freedom. In the sixth century BC the leadership of Greek culture is found on the islands. The mainland does not adopt these ideas until later. In terms of architecture it seems that stone temples were built on the islands much earlier – including very important ones on Náxos. Náxos also founds the first Greek colony on Sicily. Náxos attains its greatest influence under the ruler Lygdamis, a "tyrant" in the original, not negative sense, around 550 BC, when it already has 100,000 inhabitants.

Starting in 540 BC, the Persian Empire extends its influence to the coast of Asia Minor. Athens takes a stand and makes Délos the intellectual and cultural centre of the Attic-Delian maritime alliance. This protective league against Persia unites the Greeks in the Aegean and Asia Minor with Athens. War is unavoidable and begins in 490 BC. Already in the same year Náxos is ravaged by the Persians and is obliged to give military assistance.

The Classical Period (490–336 BC) Náxos therefore fights on the opposite side at the beginning of the Persian Wars, but is on Athens' side for the final triumph over the Persians in 449 BC. Immense riches are amassed on Délos during the "Golden Age" which follows. When Athens carries off the treasure and tries to make vassals of its allies, the islands fight against Athens in allegiance to Sparta in the Peloponnesian War, which lasts 30 years. However, Náxos is subjugated and remains a tributary of Athens until the defeat of Athens. The outcome is a forever weakened Greece. Athens loses all importance.

Hellenistic Period (338–146 BC) The Macedonians in northern Greece take over Greek culture after conquering Greece in 338 BC. For a short period Alexander the Great, a Macedonian, takes this culture, henceforth known as "Hellenism", as far as India. After his early death his world empire rapidly disintegrates into Diadochean empires, the Aegean islands being dominated by the Egyptian Ptolemies and the Antigonides from Asia Minor.

Roman Period (146 BC–395 AD) After 146 BC the Romans, as the next rulers, also make Greek culture their own, thus helping it to spread throughout Europe. Greek culture becomes that of the Occident. Délos is now one of the wealthiest places in the Empire. From Rome comes Christianity, which also becomes the state religion in the Eastern Roman Empire after 391.

The Byzantine Period (395–1204 AD) The Roman Empire is divided in 395 AD. While the Western Roman Empire is in decline after the migration of peoples in 476 AD, the eastern part of the Imperium Romanum remains an upholder of Graeco-Roman culture for 1000 years. Byzantium, the second Rome, turns eastwards, brings Christianity to the Slavs and spreads Greek ideas as far as Moscow, which later becomes known as the Second Byzantium or Third Rome.
Especially on Náxos cruciform-domed churches are built on the model of the Hagia Sophia in Constantinople. The new Islamic ideas also influence Greece in the 8th and 9th centuries. The iconoclastic controversy revolves around the admissibility of a pictorial representation of God and the Saints. The image worshipers prevail.
Europe begins to drift apart in cultural terms; the religious differences also deepen. The main points of dispute concern the Holy Ghost and the corporeal ascension of Mary, which is considered

as a "peaceful passing away" in the Orthodox Church. In 1054 the schism, or separation of the Eastern Greek-Orthodox Church from the Western Latin Church, comes about.

In these uncertain times the islands of the Aegean are often attacked by raiders such as the Vandals, the Goths, the Normans and finally the Saracens. The possibility of retreating into the interior of the island and the huge refuge fort Apalírou make Náxos a safer place than smaller islands. It isn't until the 9th century that Byzantium can consolidate its power once again.

Now, however, in the wake of the Persians, Avars and Arabs, a new Asian power has assembled on the eastern borders of Byzantium: the Turkish Seljuks. They push westward with immense force. In 1095 the Eastern Roman Empire requests help from Pope Urban II, and the crusades begin. During the fourth crusade one of the most short-sighted campaigns in history is initiated. Due to trade rivalries Venice induces the crusaders to plunder and occupy the Byzantine capital, Constantinople, in 1204. The quadriga on San Marco square is part of the loot. Not until 1261 do the Byzantians conquer the city again with the aid of the Genoans, thus terminating the Venetians' "Latin Empire". Byzantium is too weak to ever recover again and is conquered by the Turks in 1453.

The Era of the Knights   (1204–1537) For most of the Cycladic islands the domination of influential Venetian families begins after the sack of Constantinople. In Náxos these are the Sanudis and then the Crispis, who build fortified family seats, the pýrgi, in the interior of the island and bolster Catholicism.

But the Turkish-Ottoman Empire directs all its energy towards conquering Europe. After the fall of Rhodes in 1523, the Turks push on further west. In 1537 they conquer all the Cycladic islands apart from Tínos.

The Turkish Era   (1537–1830) The Fall of Constantinople in 1453 marks the end of the thousand-year-old advanced Roman-Greek civilisation. Learned Byzantine fugitives bring the Greek way of thinking back to the West again, paving the way for the Renaissance. From this time on the fortune of the Orthodox Church is determined in Moscow, which assumes the Byzantine double-headed eagle as its state coat of arms.

Yet in Greece itself the Turkish influence, from diet to music, predominates for the next 350 years. This influence is still discernible today. Yet the islands partly enjoy greater freedom. The

Turks are chiefly interested in obtaining revenue, even allowing the Jesuits to build a monastery ②. The Orthodox Church is recognised by the Turks as a mediator between government and population and proves to be the protector of Greek culture during this period.

Pan-Slavism under Catherine the Great seeks to bring the Balkan Slavs into the Russian fold. The Turkish-Russian war of 1768 to 1774 extends as far as the Aegean, where a Russian fleet occupies Náxos and 17 Cycladic islands for four years; they later return to Turkish rule.

Independent Greece   (since 1821) In 1821 the insurrection against the Turks begins on the Peloponnesus as Turkey has been weakened after another war against Russia. Europe reflects on its cultural roots. Philhellenists from many countries support the Greek struggle for independence, the Great Powers in Europe help diplomatically, and Greece becomes part of Europe again. The Cyclades are part of Greece from the outset, unlike the islands off the Turkish coast.

Twentieth Century   Greece tries to regain possession of its former settlements from the "sick man on the Bosporus". During the 1912-13 Balkan wars and the First World War several islands and Ottoman areas on the northern coast of the Aegean are occupied. After the First World War, among whose losers is Turkey, the Greeks start a war over the former areas in Asia Minor. But Turkey, emboldened once again by the "Young Turk Revolution", utterly destroys the Greeks, who then have to agree to a major population exchange.

In 1940 fascist Italy vainly attempts to occupy the country, whereupon German troops advance across the Balkans to Greece. They hand the country over to the Italians as conquered territory, but then occupy it themselves after Mussolini's fall in 1943. 70 German soldiers are stationed on Náxos. In October 1944, following a three-day battle, they surrender to the British.

After World War II   With Western help during the civil war from 1945 to 1949, Greece avoids the fate of the other Balkan countries, and doesn't disappear behind the Iron Curtain. However economic difficulties cause many to leave their native island and emigrate to Europe, the USA and Australia.

In 1981 Greece joins the EU. Its subsidies lead to an improvement in the infrastructure and facilitate a growth in tourism.

Translation of special words for hikers

English	Español	Italiano	Nederlands	Svenska
boulder	peña	masso	Rotsblok	klippblock
cairn	marcación	segnalato di pietre	Markeringssteen	vägmärke
cleft	foso	fosso	Sloot	sänka
crest	loma	dorsale	Bergkam	bergskam
culvert	corriente d.ag.	passagio	water buis	vattenledning
defile	camino hondo	strada incassata	holleweg	hålväg
dip	depresión	depressione	Glooiing	sänka
ditch	foso	fosso	Sloot	sänka
ford	vado	guado	doorwaadbare Pl.	vadställe
fork	bifurcación	bifurcazione	Wegsplitsing	vägskäl
furrow	foso	fosso	Sloot	grav
gap	brecha	breccia	Bres	inskärning
clearing	calvero	radura	Open plek in bos	glänta
gorge	garganta	abisso	Kloof	ravin
gravel	guijos	ghiaia	Steengruis	stenskärvor
grove	bosquecillo	bosco	Bosschage	lund
heath	brezal	brughiera	Heide	hed
hollow	depresión	depressione	Glooiing	sänka
incline	falda	pendio	Helling	sluttning
incision	foso	fosso	Sloot	sänka
juniper	enebro	ginepro	jeneverstruik	enbuske
past	junto a	accanto a	naast	jämte
pebble	guijarro	ciottolo	Kiezel	grus
pen	aprisco	stalla ovile	Stal	stall
ravine	garganta	abisso	Ravijn	ravin
rim	borde	orlo	Rand	kant
ridge	cresta	cresta	Bergkam	bergskam
rubble	rocalla	ditriti	Steengruis	stenar
saddle	collado	sella	Bergrug	bergsrygg
schist	pizarra	scisto	leisteen	skiffer
scree	rocalla	ditriti	Steengruis	stenar
scrub	maleza	sterpaglia	Doornbos	snår
slope	ladera	pendio	Helling	sluttning
stream-bed	corriente secco	letto di fiume	Waterloop	vattendrag
strenuous	penoso	faticoso	inspannend	ansträngande
trail	sendero	sentiero	Pad	stig
turn off	bifurcación	biforcazione	Afslag	avtagsväg
well	pozo	pozzo	Bron	brunn

German version ISBN 978-3-9808802-8-2

April in Naxos

❶ Ypsilís Castle

After a swim on the nice sandy beach of Amíti this four-hour hike leads back along country lanes. The not very varied route takes you past the abandoned Ypsiloteras castle.
If you do not want to finish early, but walk as far as Náxos town, you use the asphalt road for 20 minutes. Your efforts are then rewarded with a wonderful view across the town!
■ 7/13 km, difference in altitude 120/160 m, easy/moderate

AWT	Should there be no bus, you can take a taxi to **Galíni** (or
0.00	straight to the beach). From Galíni a little concrete road takes you through fields with vegetables to the broad
0.25	**Amíti sandy beach.** It can be polluted when there is a north wind.

The way back commences at the small beach chapel. Passing reed-lined vegetable fields ▯, you proceed to where

!!	the concrete path starts to climb. There, on the right besi-
0.40	de a steel gate, an acute-angled **sandy track** leads *backwards* uphill. Following the serpentines, you soon reach
0.50	(without using the one-way road on the right) the **Pýrgos Ypsilís** ▯, which lies embedded above some gardens.

Should the Pýrgos (14th century) be closed, you can steal a glance into a vaulted passage leading into an inner courtyard through the perforated door decorated with ironwork. The upper floor (formerly two) leans against the exterior wall and contains the stately living room of the Venetian noble family. After that monks occupied the

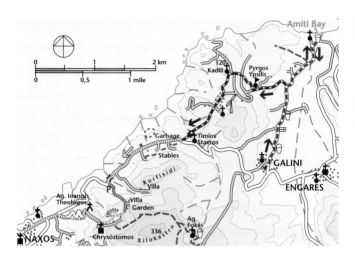

*enormous building. Ghibelline merlons and, as a special
feature, a round tower are all that remain of the erstwhile
fortifications. During sieges the ancillary buildings lying
outside were surrendered.*

On the far side of the Pýrgos you wander straight on and
1.05 up Kadíli hill to a **crossroads.** In the west you catch sight
of Páros. Now you take the level roadway to the left. Past
several complexes with holiday houses you drop below
1.25 the windmills and down to the **road** where the chapel of
Tímios Stavrós stands.

> **Short cut:** Whoever wants to avoid the asphalt road, as
> well as the steep incline and climb over a fence,
> should hail a taxi here, but at the price of then mis-
> sing an unforgettable sunset.

When you go along the asphalt road to the right, you first
find farmsteads and barns on the left, and on the right the
refuse dump. Then you march downhill into a narrow
1.45 valley with a **bridge** (**P1:** N 37°06.915′/ E 25°23.728′, 80 m).
Shortly afterwards you go up to the left on a steep
roadway to a holiday house. Below a reed-covered garden
you turn right and then left up to a basketball basket.
From here diagonally to the right and over a fence, then
on without a path. Below two farmhouses (left) and the
gate to their driveway you swing in the direction of the
2.10 **Chrisóstomos Convent** ③. However, the fortress-like

building from the 17th/18th century is not accessible.

2.20 You walk down the road, taking care not to miss the **Grotto Chapel** of St. John 4 at the first bend on the right. Here you can enjoy the sunset over the town and temple gateway, finishing up the last water rations in the process. Later you can shorten the loops in the road in order to

2.35 reach the **town beach** faster.

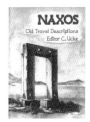

In 1984 the Munich physicist Christian Ucke wrote the first hiking book on Náxos and in 2003, together with Dieter Graf, published a revised and extended version. His rich knowledge of Náxos has also been incorporated into this new book; many thanks.

In addition, he has compiled a collection of *Old Travel Descriptions* from the 18th to the 20th century which is worth reading; it is sold in the bookshop *To Palió Bibliopolío* at the old market. (Το Παλιό Βιβλιοπωλείο)

❷ The green valley of Potamiá

The magnificent hike from Melanés to "Kouros" bus station lasts four hours, so you should take a taxi at 10 am to Melanés (about € 7,–). If you have a hire car, you can go on a five-hour ramble round Melanés. It is also possible to end the tour after two-and-a-half hours in Potamiá and return by bus. Part of the route runs along one of the finest monopátia on Náxos. Nestling in the varied farmland with many olive groves are the ruins of a Catholic monastery and the ancient marble quarry of Flério with two large, half-finished marble statues. A shady garden inn and several wells are also to be found.

■ *10 km, difference in altitude 150 m, moderate*

AWT 0.00 To the right of the "Agkor" taverna at the **bus stop in Melanés** you enter the alley and later, to the right of the "Vasilis" taverna, go up the steps – eagerly eyed by huge colourful roosters. The village's many inns specialize in chicken and rabbit dishes. At the end of the village you

0.05 come to a **bend in the road** and go up right. Down on the left stands the new church. Rising above are ornate terraces, in spring covered in luscious green ①, and above them again the white marble mountains of Kinídaros.

After three minutes you turn left into a country lane and, after a further five minutes, left again at a fork. At the fork with the signposts (**P1:** N 37°05.011'/ E25°26.307') you proceed right on the same level and, after 100 m, down right at the next sign ②. You walk past a coop (right, hens

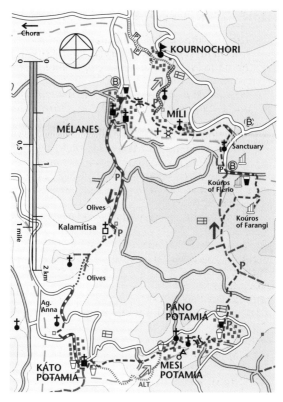

of course) and march down to the valley alongside an olive grove. Round a bend you suddenly see a large building ③ below the roadway. Hesitantly you enter the ruins of the **Jesuit Monastery Kalamítsia** (**P2:** N 37° 04.705'/ E25°26.260', 135 m).

0.25

> *From the 17th century, on what was then Osman Náxos, the Jesuits ran a monastery and large estates, but this led to tensions with the local farmers. Travellers were always welcome as guests of the monastery that existed until 1927.*
>
> *Today one first enters the tall refectory, with reception rooms on either side. The monastic cells are in the lower building at the back.*

In the prolongation of the country lane there is a path for

0.30 hikers which leads uphill, then downhill, before dividing behind a walled enclosure. We go **left downhill**, later to the right of the overgrown path. Further down well-beat-

0.40 en paths run through an olive grove to the **road.** There, at the "doorbell", we go through a gate and up left, but only for four minutes! In the first sharp left-hand bend we leave the road and go right, along the fence of the Anna Chapel, and down a mule track. Then, further down at some ruins, left down to a concrete track and left up this

0.55 to the large church of **Káto Potamiá** (85 m). Below it lies the nice garden inn of a hobby innkeeper. Then we follow a lane up the valley for three minutes as far as a fork above a manhole cover.

> **Alternative:** Walking downhill one comes to the ruin of the Kokkos Pýrgos (see p. 54). At AWT 1.10 one returns to the main route (see below).

★ Climbing up to the left, we find a beautiful old mule track lined by walls. A short way along a road, then straight ahead at the steps (right) on to a footpath. On the left in

1.10 **Mési Potamiá** is a **well.** (This is where we are rejoined by the alternative route.)

Further up the hill we turn left off the broad cobbled path and struggle up steps (see p. 54 ④) leading to a chapel (left). At the top we descend again immediately to the

1.15 right, past a small **chapel** with an overlapping stone slab roof (right).

Proceeding along the shady stream, we later climb up to

!! the right until *in front* of the old stone steps. Here we walk left on the level, along the main alley in **Páno Potamiá**

1.20 (Odos Giampoúra) as far as the **Platía Orphanoú** – really just a widening of the street. At the far end we swing

down left. On the left at the well lies the popular garden inn "Pigí", the source. In case anyone has overlooked it: **P3:** N37°04.209'/ E25°26.981', 170 m.

Leaving the garden, we head straight on, to the right of the source, car park and church, in to the narrow alley leading up to the road, which we cross (sign "Flerio").

★ Then, at the cemetery (left), begins one of the most beautiful mule tracks on Náxos ④. Although traversed by a concrete track, it continues, displaced 20 m to the left.

1.35 The path reaches a **fork** (**P4:** N37°04.512'/ E25°27.049'). Here we follow the sign "Kouros" to the left. Above a dip we saunter gaily between olive trees as far as the highest point of the hike at 245 m. Some distance away on the right we can make out the quarried marble mountains of Kinídaros. At a fork we turn right and, after a right-hand bend, recognize the walled-in site with visitors on the op-

1.55 posite slope ⑤. Passing to the right through a **gap in the wall** we later go down to the entrance. Up until five years

2.00 ago the **Koúros of Farangi** (or Potamiá) lay hidden between the bushes (see p.58 ④) – the privilege of seeing it was not granted to many.

> *"Kouroi" are larger-than-life ancient sculptures of standing youths. These two here were destined for shrines, but were never finished due to material defects.*

The cobbled path leads down to the dry-bed and there to the left. At the second gap in the wall, 40 m further down,

2.10 can be found the other sculpture, the **Koúros of Flério** ⑥. And beside it a modest garden inn.

Back on the concrete track, we walk left and, before the large car park in the dip, up to the right – a cobbled path commences after about 50 m.

*It is possible to walk on up to the fork in the road and visit the new archaeological excavation of the **shrine of the stonemasons**. This is a round site with a diameter of forty metres which was dedicated to a goddess of fertility, whose two sons were the patron saints of the stonemasons. During antiquity this shrine belonged to the quarry.* Further up, you can catch the **bus** at 2.30 pm and drive home. To be sure, have a look at the bus sign, for it may stop further down.

2.15 If one takes the said cobbled path to the left along the slope, one soon comes below **Ipapánti Chapel.** After a section fit for traffic, the path plunges in to the green valley, where huge cactus figs form a guard of honour.

Below the houses in **Míli** one strolls on and drops down left in front of a house blocking the way. Standing in the gardens on the left are three old water mills. Here our stepped path is accompanied by a gully. Next comes a

2.30 **wayside altar** on the left. After the last house in Míli (left, with external staircase) begins the stepped path into the valley (**P5:** N37°05.302'/ E25°26.538', 160 m). On the

2.45 other side of the valley we head up to **Melanés**, where our hire car is waiting.

▶ **The long-distance trail N1** is marked with yellow signs. See the website www.naxos.gr > Hiking. The five stages are:
1. Chóra – Angídia - Melanés
2. Melanés – Ano Potamiá – Chalkí
3. Chalkí – Filóti – Fotodótis – Apíranthos
4. Apíranthos – Kóronos - Skadó
5. Skadó – Mési – Apóllonas

❸ To the dunes of Pláka

From Vívlos we descend an attractive, in places somewhat overgrown path on to the fertile plain of Pláka and wander through the fields to the extensive sand dunes.
■ *6 km, difference in altitude 140 m, easy*

AWT
0.00 It does not take long to reach **Vívlos/Trípodes** by bus. In the **rift-valley** on the southern perimeter of the village, below a large church with several towers, a roadway leads us along the upper edge of the wide valley to two chapels. The first one, enclosed by a fence, is on our left as we pro-

0.15 ceed. Before the second, **St. George's Chapel** (150 m) ①, we turn left below the ruin of a watchtower and, after 60 m, down right. At the bottom the roadway runs past another chapel (right), to the right and then uphill. Lying bet-

0.20 ween the rocks is the **grotto chapel Agios Nikoláos (P1: N 37°03.069'/ E 25°23.900', 125 m).** The next part of the trail down to the sea is somewhat overgrown. Spread out on the right is the plain of Pláka, lush farmland with plentiful water supplies. Wine, cereals and vegetables are cultivated, but above all potatoes, a culinary delight much relished by Greek connoisseurs.

0.35 Down in the **plain** we keep to the right and encounter reed-covered paths (see p. 11 ①), which eventually lead right to a little concrete road running at right angles.

*If you follow it 250 m to the right, you come to the ruins of the **Paléopyrgos,** a Hellenic fortress-tower made of dry cut stone. These fortified rural residences were widespread in the Aegean. The tower with five to seven floors and*

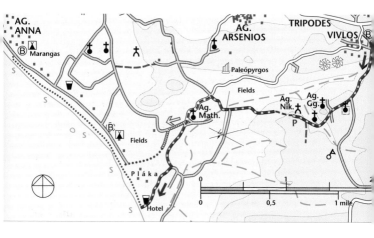

> the wall thickness of one metre afforded protection
> against assault.
> A better preserved example of this type of construction is
> Chimárrou tower ⑮.

Heading towards the sea, we then walk past two rocky
hills (right) and the buried St. Matthew's chapel ② (left,
with ancient structural parts) and arrive at a transverse
sand track. (Going right would bring us to the sea quicker,
albeit later having to cross fields without a path.) If we
follow the signs pointing left towards Mikrí Vígla, subsequently turning right to the hotel complex by the sea, we

1.10 end up on the infinite **dune beach of Pláka.** Sometimes
1.30 the bus only leaves from the **Máragas** campsite, so we
"have" to shuffle along the strand for 20 minutes.

▷ At the old market in Naxos town is an inn which differs
from the usual: "Lucullus" offers traditional island fare.

❹ The resurrected temple

This three to four-hour trek leads you to the reconstructed Temple of Demeter, which lies amid a charming landscape. On over a plateau with tilled fields, mainly along country lanes, you then come to the long sandy beach of Pláka. That is your first chance to take a rest in a taverna.

■ *11 km, difference in altitude 220 m, moderate*

AWT
0.00 We jump off the bus at the **Ano Sangrí junction** and march 500 m along the road to the village. Turning half-right at the crossroads before it, we bear left to the monument in the small pine wood, down to the concrete road and then left along a village alley to the uninhabited
0.10 monastery **Ayios Eleftérios**.

Opposite the monastery, to the right of a stone gentleman with a bow-tie, we descend the steps and wander to the right on a country lane in the direction of a hill chapel. Later the lane runs along below the chapel ①. On the left you later see a wide plain with olive trees and, opposite at an angle, the temple ② on the hill. Our lane ends above a farm shed (**P1:** N 37°02.101'/ E 25°26.056') and we follow a red arrow to the right on to a mule track. Later we drop down along a well-beaten track on the left into the hollow, go right, then left and, on the monopáti leading towards the middle of the valley, through the dry-bed. Se-
0.30 cret paths bring us to the **temple.**

*The **Temple of Demeter,** the goddess of agriculture, was built around 600 BC in the classical style. In 500 AD a Christian church with three naves was integrated, at the*

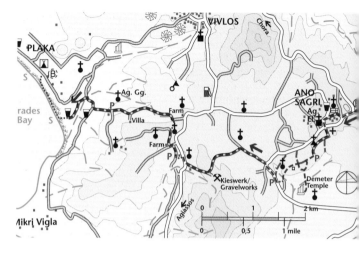

*same time turning the axis by 90°. On the south side of
the temple it is possible to make out the church's round
apsis. In front of the entrance to the temple lie the foun-
dations of a Christian monastery which was likewise
added on.*

*Using thousands of marble pieces which were lying
around, the reconstruction was completed in 2001 after
five years, together with that of a small, yet fine museum
(see p. 34).*

We return to the original path, traverse the hollow again,
come to the already familiar monopáti and go left. On our
left is the re-erected temple and we take pleasure in the
fact that an ancient temple has again become part of this

delightful landscape, in close harmony with the mountains and fields all around. A ruined house provides a suitable picnic spot from which to admire this sight.

0.40   We then trudge on through a **hollow**, which is sometimes wet in spring, immediately afterwards taking a country lane on the right and, before the olive grove, make our way up left without a trail to the saddle. Head along the

0.50   **road (P2:** N 37°01.766'/ E 25°25.505') to the right in a northerly direction. To the right lies our point of departure Ano Sangrí. At the crossing (sign in the opposite direction: Dímitras) the way leads straight on along a country lane. We are surrounded by wide fields and solitary, shady trees which have been much punished by the wind.

0.55   Now turn left at the **fork** leading over the hill which marks the boundary of the plain. On the way down, the track passes a gravel/cement works (left) and ends at the

1.20   **road.** We have to march 100 m along it to the right, until we are below a chapel on the slope (right) ③. There on the left beside the road stands the house of a liqueur manufacturer; along its lower fence we stalk cross-country for

1.30   120 m and hit upon a **country lane (P3:** N 37°02.115'/ E 25°24.162') in the hollow. Walk up it to the right. Where walls later block your path, go left and then right in front

1.40   of a **farmhouse.** A little farther on you must watch out: about 30 m to the right of the roadway stands a **miniature**

1.45   **barrel-vaulted chapel** with free-standing bell-tower.

!!   At the left-hand bend we go *straight ahead* and immediately find a rather overgrown, yet negotiable mule track.

1.50   After 200 m, beside a pasture, it meets a **roadway**, which we take to the left. Shortly afterwards we stumble across a well on the left. The way now leads through quiet coun-

2.05   tryside ④ towards the sea. Down on the **coastal plain** a roadway branches off to the left (**P4:** N 37°02.579'/ E 25°23.160') – we ignore it and come to a transverse track. Whoever is searching for an empty strand should go left here. Whoever is searching for the shortest way should go right, then left, then not into the cul-de-sac, but follow

2.15   the sign "**Beach**". What a relief to dispose of those garments!

     We tramp along the strand for twenty minutes until

2.55   reaching the **bus stop** beside the supermarket.

Temples on Náxos

Besides Délos and Páros, the only important temples of the Greek Classical Period in the Cyclades can be found on Náxos. Here, three temples have been excavated and examined. German archaeologists played an important role in these excavations.

The Temple to **Apóllon on the Palátia peninsula,** with its mighty portal (page 4), greeting all visitors, has never been completed. The previous construction there had also been dedicated to Apóllon, the god of light. Temples dedicated to Apóllon facing Délos existed on several islands. Every year there was a great festival, and, simultaneously, celebrations took place on the surrounding islands. In clear weather, it was probably possible to see the light signals from the holy island.

Around 530 BC the tyrant Lýgdamis started building the temple, which is still clearly recognisable today. With exterior measurements of 24 x 55 m and a pillar height of about 13 m, it would have become one of the largest temples of those days. The portal, which has an unusual depth and was set 1.20 m above the ground, was possibly used as a stage for political purposes or oracles. The actual entrance was located at the side. 1000 years later, the temple was transformed into an early-Christian basilica and another 1000 years later, it was used as a quarry for the Chóra by the Venetians.

The **Temple to Demeter in Sangrí** ⑤ ⑧ was discovered by the Greek archaeologist N. Kontoleon in 1949. He noticed the great number of architectural fragments in the isolated chapel of Saint John. Together with some farmers, he located the first pieces. His later excavation in 1954 and especially the German-Greek excavation between 1976 and 1995 proved the uniqueness of this rural Ionic temple. Its size was 12.6 x 13.2 m, and, except for two wooden doors, it was completely out of marble. No signs of an altar were found. There were two identical side entrances from the entrance-hall, the *Pronaos* in the main room and a windowless *Cella.* The roof was covered with marble tiles 2–4 cm thick which allowed the light to shine through from above! The cult chamber also had another special characteristic: walls that had been left in their original rough condition. When the doors were shut, one had the feeling of being in a cave. This leads to the assumption that celebrations to the earth and fertility goddesses Démeter and Kore took place here at night, until the first daylight came through the ceiling of the room. Cavities for sacrificial offerings, hewn into the stone platform in front of the temple, also prove that Démeter was worshipped.

During several reconstruction measures to build the church, the exterior wall of the temple was taken away around 500 AD, and, in addition to the basilica, a small cloister with an inner courtyard was added.

The tremendous accomplishment of archaeologists and architects consisted in being able to visualise the ancient temple and the early-medieval basilica among approximately 1600 fragments scattered all over, some of which had even been built into the walls of farmhouses. Then the chapel of Saint John was taken apart and moved aside, and the temple was put together as a puzzle with the original marble fragments and the others new. The contour of the basilica is visible again. All these efforts have been supported by funds from the European Union, which are certainly much better invested here than in some of the other measures regarding infrastructure.

The **Temple to Diónysos of Iría** south of the city was discovered by G. Gruben and V. Lambrinudakis in 1986. The approximate site had been known from reports. After intensive questioning of some of the farmers in the potato fields, the right spot could be located. Excavations revealed four levels of temples exactly on top of each other. The most recent, the upper level, had measurements of 13 x 29 m and was in a walled-in sanctuary measuring 100 x 60 m. Nowhere can the development of the Cycladic temples between the 8th and 5th centuries BC and of the Diónysos cult be seen better. The excavation field has now been covered again and secured. It may be visited, but very little is recognisable.

⑤ The land of Demeter

This three to four-hour round trip follows country lanes and footpaths through fields and groves round the ruins of the temple of the goddess of fertility, Demeter. The green undulating plain has no wells to offer, but Ano Sangrí has a taverna.
■ *8 km, difference in altitude 100 m, easy to moderate*

AWT From the **bus stop in Ano Sangrí** it is 500 m to the cross-
0.00 roads before the village. On the right is the sports field.
0.05 Diagonally opposite the bus shelter at the **crossing** our country lane leads down left. Embedded in the mountains on the left you can see the village of Moní. 200 to 300 m further a chapel tries to hide in the reeds on the right ①. 200 m beyond a farmhouse with "pasture" (left)
0.15 the old Byzantine church **Ioánnis o Theólogos** comes into view on the right. It contains frescoes from the 11th to 13th centuries, but is unfortunately closed.

Continuing straight ahead on the lane, ahead of us we be-
0.20 hold the fertile plain of Sangrí. Ignore a **branch-off** to the right (**P1:** N37°02.078'/ E25°26.474') and climb slightly. At a fork in front of a ruined house we bear right and, 200 m further (100 m before a white chapel), turn down right
0.25 on to a **narrow lane.** Shortly after the dry-bed we ascend to the left (**P2:** N37°01.939'/ E25°26.293') The monopáti which now follows is rather overgrown. After a fence, opened by lifting, we walk on a mule track – first on the level, then down left towards a grey chapel ② which, hidden a little by trees, waits above the dip.

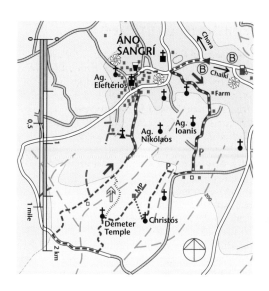

0.35 *The cruciform-domed* **Christós Chapel** *was for a long time a deserted ruin. Now it again possesses a few simple pictures and, in the chancel, the remains of frescoes of saints.*

★ On the side with the entrance a wide doorway opens on to a picnic place beneath an olive tree. Quite a few of these gnarled old trees stand in the meadow across which we subsequently tramp uphill without a path. At the top our way is crossed by a monopáti, which we take to the left, past a new house. Behind the house we follow the ruts until, all of a sudden, we find ourselves standing in front of a dappled temple ③.

0.45 *The lighter marble blocks were added during reconstruction in 2001. More about the* **Temple of Demeter** *on page 34.*

 Short cut: The way through the dip below the temple is described on pp. 31 and 32.

To be able to take in the wonderful position of the former temple, though, one ought to ramble round it after the visit. To do so, descend the over-width footpath to the car 0.50 park and walk right on the **road.** After six minutes a wooden sign points you to the right through a dip, which however is often damp in spring.

There you reach a beautiful footpath ④, which reveals the exalted position of the temple on the right. A little later a
1.15 **monopáti** leads down right – the short cut described above. But you go straight on and come on to a country
1.25 lane, which later veers left to **Ano Sangrí.**

Past the Eleftérios monastery (left) you walk through an alley to the road. There you go right and in an arc round the garishly painted taverna, before proceeding right up the steps to the small pine wood with war memorial. Then on to the crossroads and back 500 m again to the
1.35 bus **stop** on the main road.

Museum of Cycladic Art in Athens

Starting from Syntagma Square, it is a five-minute walk along Vasilissis Sofias Street to the Museum of *Cycladic & Ancient Greek Art* in Neofitou Douka St. 4.

This private museum has the most comprehensive collection of Cycladic idols on an area of 2,000 m2.

On display here are about 350 exhibits from what is the oldest civilization in Europe as well as finds from the Neolithic and Hellenistic Ages. A visit to this museum is the perfect way to round off a trip to the Cyclades.

Open from 10 am to 4 pm, Saturdays until 3 pm, *closed Tuesdays and Sundays.*

⑥ Venetian pýrgi

A four-hour trek through Arcadian landscapes to Filóti. Walk along the old main path through the island, protected by ancient tower-houses or pýrgi. These medieval fortress-towers were the easily defensible country residences of the Venetian nobility. About 30 such towers still exist on Naxos.
■ *9 km, altitude difference 160 m, easy to moderate*

AWT

0.00

It's best to tell the bus driver where you want to get off shortly before you get there, i.e. **Káto Sangrí**. (There is a marble factory on the left, just before the road turns off to K.S.). The bus stops at a stone **bus shelter** (left) opposite the road to Káto Sangrí. You follow the disappearing bus for 200 m along the road, leaving it at a right bend and turning on to a country lane straight ahead in the direction of Mt. Zás ①. There is a power line on the left. (The bus frequently stops almost next to this turn-off on the road leading off right to Kanakári!)

On the way down, you see the first inhabited pýrgos (Paléologos ②) against the backdrop of Apáno Kástro, the main Venetian fortress in the hinterland of the island ⑨.

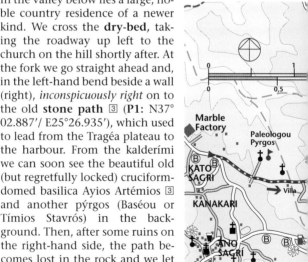

0.15

In the valley below lies a large, noble country residence of a newer kind. We cross the **dry-bed**, taking the roadway up left to the church on the hill shortly after. At the fork we go straight ahead and, in the left-hand bend beside a wall

!!

0.20

(right), *inconspicuously right* on to the old **stone path** ③ (**P1**: N37° 02.887'/ E25°26.935'), which used to lead from the Tragéa plateau to the harbour. From the kalderími we can soon see the beautiful old (but regretfully locked) cruciform-domed basilica Ayios Artémios ③

★

and another pýrgos (Baséou or Tímios Stavrós) in the background. Then, after some ruins on the right-hand side, the path becomes lost in the rock and we let

0.30   ourselves be guided by the wall on the left to a **country lane.**

After passing a polygonal building, you come to the main

0.35   road. Proceeding left along it for 50 m, you find a **country lane** on the left, later a footpath which runs below the road to Ephraim chapel. Here you cross the road and enter a track. After about 200 m two mule tracks branch off

0.40   to the left. We take the *second* **path**, which leads straight ahead between walls (**P2:** N37°03.055'/ E25°27.774').

We are now on the fertile Tragéa plain with its large olive groves. High walls on our right lead us safely through,

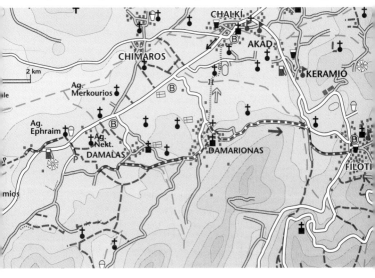

0.50	past the small village of **Damalás** in the hollow, protected by an attractive domed church. We hike on to the village
1.00	of **Damariónas.** Right at the start of the village, at the corner of a house ④, we head into a maze of alleys, passing the church (right), turning right before an archway
1.05	and then down to the overgrown **war memorial** on the asphalt road.

Alternative: The way to Filóti described below is asphalted from here. You can reach **Chalkí via small mule tracks** in 15 minutes: Descend *15 steps* to the left of the memorial (not of the statue!), go right at the fork which follows immediately and later left in front of a low wall. Go to the right behind the small bridge and then turn left again directly afterwards, passing the sports field on your right and going through the narrow pass. Then, keeping left of the houses, you'll arrive at the washing facilities in Chalkí.

The way to Filóti leads up to the right of the monument.

| 1.10 | At the **junction**, you bear left and are soon at the upper end of the Tragéa plain on a road with a great view, surrounded by olive trees. No matter how hard you try, you will not lose your way here and thus have all the time in the world to look out for more pýrgi. Three can be seen at once – two in Chalkí and one in Keramío. |

Below Filóti we take the bridge over the hollow, then the track right directly after and later wander up to the left, between gardens beneath Mt. Zás, to the inviting street cafés

| 1.30 | of **Filóti.** The patrons know exactly when the next bus will arrive and that there is still time to stop for refreshment under the plane trees. If you're interested, you will also find a pýrgos south of the main church here in Filóti. |

❼ Into the plain of Tragéa

An easy trek to whet your appetite, through the olive groves of the Tragéa plateau. Two and a half hours over easily identifiable tracks and paths with a pleasant stop at a taverna in Chalkí.

■ *6 km, difference in altitude 60 m, easy*

AWT The most difficult part comes straightaway: explaining to
0.00 the driver that you want to get off at the **turning to Agiassós** (or Tímios Stávros). Here you head along the road between the petrol station and the windmills, up to
0.05 the bulky, unadorned **Tímios Stávros** (i.e. "true cross", also called **Pýrgos Baséou**).

> *This Venetian castle residence from 1671 was later a monastery and is now a regional cultural centre (p.46). Spread out below is a fertile plain, which reaches right down to the sea – and is watched over by the Temple of Demeter, the goddess of fertility.*

Directly behind the monastery a roadway ascends over slabs of rock in to the olive groves. You wander along cheerfully – to your left the wide valley protected by the Venetian castle up on the highest mountain. Then turn
0.15 right at the fork to the **reservoir.**

The track leading past the olive groves is lined by nut bushes ①. In September, preparations are made for the olive harvest: tightly woven nets are spread beneath the trees ② and in November the ripe olives are knocked off. At some turnings to the right wander straight down in to
0.25 the **hollow**, where you come across an attractive paved stone path through a field (**P1: N 37°05.979′/ E 25°**

32.374'). Bear right ahead of the fence, down in to the already familiar shady lane and walk left.

0.30 From a **small hill** you look across the beautiful plain of Tragéa, which remains green all year.

The torso of a windmill is visible left on a hill; we march on unwaveringly below it, on what is now a concrete track which makes a left-hand bend - at this very spot we take the second path to the right up to the small church

0.35 **Ayios Nektários** on the hilltop ③ with its fine view. If you prefer not to take a break here, continue downhill along the track, taking in the attractive, green surroundings as you go. On the right, between some trees, you have a view of the hamlet Damalás and, above in the distance, you see the mountain village

0.40 Moní. When you come to the **bridge** alongside a chapel, turn right on the road and, 50 m further on, bear left on to a roadway lined by ancient olive trees. Later, then, at the fork after a chapel (right), we naturally take the more attractive way down left into a dry-bed, right there for 30

0.50 m before going up a few steps to **Chímarros** and the road. Here, the relentless Cycladic wanderers among us head uphill past the cemetery, turning right at the washing

1.00 area at the small church of **Tsikalarió** before heading
down again, contentedly, over a splendid paved path and
left on the roadway below.

> *Short cut:* The others forgo Tsikalarío and, 400 m fur-
> ther on, turn off left into this roadway between a shed
> and a chapel.

You take this roadway for only 50 m and turn down right
into the dry-bed at some markings. On the other side is a
sunken path leading to Chalkí.

> ▶ From a three-way junction one could follow the
> signs left before the edge of the village and, in five
> minutes, reach the beautiful church **Ayios Geórgios
> o Diassorítis** (George the Rescuer) ④, an attractive
> example of a Byzantine cruciform-domed basilica of
> the Tragéa with valuable frescoes inside.

Keeping right at the first houses in **Chalkí** (290 m), we
1.10 take a look at the **platía** to see who else is lolling around
in front of Jannis' taverna.

Later on, you can get the bus at the church of Protótronis
with its superb interior.

➑ The Byzantine Castle Apalírou

The six to seven-hour tour leads through a barren region to the ruins of the enormous Byzantine castle on the 474 m high Apalírou. For a good deal of the way there is no path between the rocks, where one should be sure-footed. The short cut, on the other hand, a three to four-hour tour with cave churches, does not require much experience in path-finding – for it mostly follows country lanes. In both cases one comes across a well.

■ *10 km, difference in altitude 130 m, moderate*
■ *16 km, difference in altitude 250 m, difficult*

AWT 0.00   On the bus to Chalkí it is best to sit near the driver and ask him to stop at the **branch-off to Agiassós**; there you will see a petrol station on the left. Walking past it up beside the windmills (right), you come to **Pýrgos Baséou**.

0.05

> *The name recalls the owners in the 19th century, the equally usual name **Tímios Stavrós** ("true cross") the times when it was a monastery (p. 43).*

Now you go down the road and, after 150 m, 20 m before the roadway, turn left on to a footpath, which is difficult to make out at first. Further up it runs immediately to the left of the field wall, before rising to tall ruins in the rocks. Having reached the ruins of a former monastery after 15 minutes and 100 metres in altitude, you discover something very special in them:

0.20

> *The **Cave Church Kalorítsa**, the "propitious Mother of God" ①, whose history goes back to the 4th century BC. From the outside it is possible to look in to the closed*

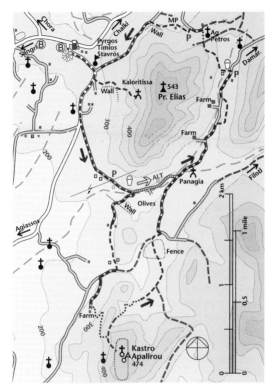

church, which houses very valuable mural paintings. During Turkish rule it was a secret school, in which the children were taught religion and the Greek alphabet by monks.

Take the same path down in to the valley as far as the
0.35 **road**, where you turn left. Shortly afterwards you leave it
0.40 again **to the left** and stroll on along a country lane. In your walking direction appears a towering, cone-shaped mountain. Our destination, oh dear! To the left of it, on the horizon, rises up Mt. Zeus with its distinctive steep drop.

We are joined by a power line (**P1:** N 37°01.696'/ E
0.50 25°27.106'). Down on the right is a **pump**, a second one (left) later offers a water tap. This is where the tour to Apalírou castle branches off to the right.

Short cut: The climb to the castle is largely without a path – sure-footedness and a sense of orientation are required. If you want to take a short cut, proceed another seven minutes along the previous roadway as far as the second right turn of a roadway. Hidden here on the right in a dry-bed is the cave church Panagía (AWT 3.10 ④).

The conquerors of the castle ascend from the pump through the gully and right up the country lane. After a wide gate the vehicle tracks ② pass through tall juniper bushes and end near some sheds. A path leads us on between these, then makes a short swing to the left. Running 1.05 beside a fence as far as **house ruins**, it ends at a walled-in grove. From there a country lane takes us right. At a VW-van-cum-chicken-shack we turn up left and 1.10 come to a small **farmhouse**.

Up on the left a proud sign marks the beginning of the way to the kástro. But one should not try too hard to find it: it only consists of goat tracks. Go up it, keeping to the right. Further up, stay about 100 m to the left above a saddle 1.35 where, after traversing the crest, you come to a **path**, which is little easier to follow – first right and later reaching 2.00 ing the defence wall of **Kástro Apalírou** ③.

The kástro was the island's main fortress at least from the 8th century. After the Byzantines were ejected by the Genoese, the latter had to defend themselves against the Venetians in 1207. Following a five-month siege Marco Sanudo became ruler of Náxos. He built his own castle, the Apáno Kástro, and left this edifice to decay.

The castle's field of ruins has the gigantic dimensions of 350 x 50 to 90 metres. The position of the doorways is

not known. Only a small part of the defence wall is left, it is easier to make out the remains of a few defence towers. In the ruins of the actual building it is easiest to recognize the cisterns, smoothed inside with reddish, clayey plaster. The chapel is from a later date. The view across the island is extremely rewarding.

2.00 To descend, use the familiar path, which later (at AWT 1.35 on the way up) swings right to the north-east into the cultivated dip. It peters out a little further down – not

2.45 until on the **valley floor** do you find more recognizable tracks again. In front of a fence you go left until in front

2.50 of a **wall with fence** at the foot of the hill.

From there you stalk to the right on a well-beaten path through juniper bushes. About 40 m to the right of the wall with fence you come to an opening in the wire and later, at the black water water pipe, to another opening. Here two fences two metres apart form a footpath, which

3.00 you take to the right as far as a **country lane.** (To the right it leads, initially across a deserted rocky valley, to Filóti in 1¼ hours.)

We go left into a dry-bed. Hidden there on the right, a few

3.10 metres further up, is the plain **Cave Church of the Panagía** ④. It is dedicated to the Mother of God.

On the other side of the dry-bed go up right on a wide

3.20 roadway. On the left soon comes a large **farmhouse**, where you leave the previous roadway by going right for a while and can walk parallel above it. Later you have to return to the austere roadway again.

3.30 But running down to the left from it is a **wide path** *across rock slabs* (**P2**: N 37°02.394'/ E 25°28.015'). In the hollow stand two houses and, further right, up at the foot of Mt. Elias, is a barrel-vaulted chapel. Descend here, then ascend on the right through the hollow. Above a cattle trough (left) you see the portal to a deserted house with nice old plasterwork. Pass it on a monopáti, which then branches right, runs along on the level for a while and

3.40 then, to the left of a fence, leads up to **Petros Chapel** with barrel-vaulted roof.

Thereafter you proceed over the hill without a path to a transverse, overgrown monopáti and turn left before it. Keeping the newish little farmhouse down to your right, you drop to the right on a country lane.

Later on the left, running parallel to the lane between the

trees, is the old footpath, which you now take instead
(**P3:** N 37°02.566'/ E 25°27.808'). It initially runs across a
3.50   meadow, but then, after a **shed** (left), becomes a beautiful
sunken path and finally crosses a roadway. Here you go
left and, at Pýrgos Tímios Stávros, down the street to the
4.15   right to the **main road**, where the bus will hopefully
soon come whizzing down.

Bus journey times from Náxos town:
Chalkí 25, Filóti 30, Apíranthos 45 minutes, Kóronos 1hr.
Koronída 1hr.20, Apóllonas 1hr.45.
Timetables can be picked up at Chóra bus station.
Tickets are always sold near to bus stops – never by the bus
driver! If you want to board a bus along the route, it is wise to
have a ticket with you. Otherwise however the driver will also
let one rectify the omission at the next point of sale.

Taxi numbers: Chóra 6974-410723, 6944-845269
Filóti 6977-939321 **Koronída** 6944-705863, 6977-467889

⑨ Apáno Kástro, the Venetian fortress

Mainly following mule tracks, we wander across the extremely verdant valley of Potamiá in four to five hours. The very beautiful tour then leads on past the Venetian fortress to Chalkí. Water abounds everywhere and Áno Potamiá has a pleasant garden taverna to offer as well. Please enquire about where to alight from the bus in advance!

■ *10 km, difference in altitude 270 m, moderate*

AWT   On the bus to Chalkí you had better sit beside the driver and tell him that you want to get off beyond Galanádo (Greek: *metaxy* Galanádo), above Ágios Mámas (Thélo na katevó amésos metá ton Ágio Máma?).

Three minutes beyond Galanádo stands a concrete factory on the left, later a filling station. Some 400 m farther on the road leads over a pass (unfinished building on the right) from where you can see another valley and numerous peaks to the left. This is our stop!!

From here you can survey the route of the hike: the three parts of Potamiá can be seen in the green fold of the slope opposite and, on the steep cliffs to the right above, our destination – Apáno Kástro.

0.00   In the **saddle** ① an initially inconspicuous path runs into the valley (straight on at the fork). Soon you behold a barrel-vaulted chapel on the right and later the old church of

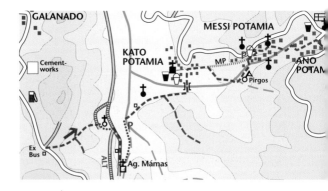

Ayios Mámas . Right at the bottom take a few steps to the right along the path running crosswise.

0.12   As the **portal** has long since been bolted, simply climb over the wall and continue down to the empty barrel-vaulted chapel without a trail. Turn right along the roadway below.

> *Alternative:* If you do not wish to clamber over the wall, go left on the roadway and then right at a sharp bend farther down.

> *After a few metres you come to the ruins of the seat of the archbishop built in 1707 and, farther down, to the picturesque ruins of the cruciform-domed basilica of **Áyios Mámas**. Built in the 9th century, it was the main church on the island as well as being, during Venetian rule, the seat of the Catholic archbishop.*

0.20

From here we follow the wooden signposts to the bottom of the valley. On the other side we can pick out the next

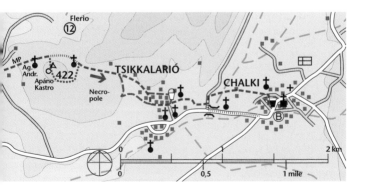

leg of our route ③, a monopáti in front of ruins. In the
0.25   **ditch** (**P1:** N 37°03.770′/ E 25°25.729′) we go uphill and
continue along a splendid path through olive groves. This
rich agricultural land is dotted with cypress trees. We proceed straight on at a fork, through a hollow and up to
0.40   **Káto Potamiá.** Leaving the church (with a water tap and
adjacent garden inn) to our left, we bear right into the alley and carry on up through the village, about 200 m beyond which is a fork (above a manhole cover).

> *Alternative:* To the left is a marvellous panorama path,
> with views across the valley and its olive trees, leading
> directly up to Mési Potamiá.

Following the signs downhill, walk past the turn-off to
the closed Perivóli garden, which is hardly worth visiting.
0.50   The next turn-off takes you to the right above the **dry-
bed**, which you follow until you come to the romantic ruins of the Kokkos Pýrgos right beside the path on the
right. It is not locked, so you can walk through the vaulted rooms of differing height. The embrasures on the top
floor date back to less peaceful times.
0.55   Steps lead us to **Mési Potamiá.** At the well (**P2:** N 37°
04.116′/ E 25°26.570′) we start climbing up past another
1.00   well and up to the left to a **chapel** (left) ④. From here we
head right down and then, at an old chapel with an im-
bricated barrel-vaulted roof (right), down left before following a stream for a bit.

At a fork, a wide stepped path leads up to the right and
!!   straight ahead. After 80 m we *turn left* to the main alley
through the upper part of **Áno Potamiá.** We now need to
watch out: in the alley on the left are steps for sitting on
1.05   and on the other side a disused **well.** If you carry straight

on here, you come to the popular garden taverna "Pigí".

!!

1.10 At the well we go up the steps of the *Odos Nikolaoy Orfanoy* to the **asphalt road.** Just opposite, a roadway runs straight on up in the direction of Apáno Kástro. At a left bend (**P3:** N 37°04.013'/ E 25°27.209') the practised Cycladic eye spots a kalderími on the right which, to the left of a wall, leads up into the pass on the left-hand side of the fortress-topped mountain. 40 m beyond the small

1.25 **Andreas Chapel** you come to an opening through the wall and scramble up the slope to the right without a path

1.35 to the **Apáno Kástro.** Phew!!

> *The former main Venetian fortress used to be called Castel d'Alto – the upper fortress – in contrast to the fortress in Chóra. The rock had been inhabited since prehistoric times, as proven by ancient wall remains and burial sites. In the 13th century it was fortified anew by the Venetians (see p. 49).*

On the opposite (southern) side we climb down to the horseshoe-shaped gun turret; here was the entrance to the anterior fortress. On the left we go down to the Panteleimon chapel in the saddle, where we can use an opening to reach the other side of the wall. We now stroll across terraced fields with distant views of Mount Zeus and the Tragéa plateau stretched out in front. Further down, walking between huge rocks, we come to the village of

2.00 **Tsikkalarió.** Stay on the main alley, turning left at the bottom beside the chapel at the car park.

A green, shady footpath beneath oaks and mistletoe brings us to a fork beside the road below. If you do not care to use the road to Chalkí, go 40 paces up the roadway to the left and then right on to a marked path. First traversing a dry-bed, and then olive groves, this likewise

2.15 leads to **Chalkí** (**P4:** N37°03,749'/ E25°28,936', 260 m). Keeping to the right, you will find some tavernas to relax in while waiting for the bus.

⑩ Two old youths

The idyllic three to four-hour hike leading to two marble statues mostly does without clearly defined trails, but it is easy to find the way. You only have four-and-a-half hours between the arrival of the bus in Chalkí and the return journey from the Koúros, so be sure to enquire about bus times, also for Melanés.

■ *11 km, difference in altitude 250 m, easy to moderate*

AWT 0.00 Take the first bus to **Chalkí**, turn down the **alley** to the right of the kafeníon and go past Jannis' attractive inn. Sorry, no time today!

0.06 Head right on the road below, leaving the village, and proceed 300 m along the road between olive groves, past a chapel (right) as far as a **bridge** with a little house ①. There you follow the path to the right and, after 20 m, left up a simply idyllic path to the village **Tsikkalarió**. On the edge of the village a chapel overlooks the plain of Tragéa. A lot of the houses in this delightful area have tiled roofs because it rains relatively frequently here. The way

0.18 through the village is fairly flat. At the **end of the village**, in the midst of a moon landscape, you see the ruins of the mountain fortress Apáno Kástro and come to a wall in the green valley above.

Alternative: If you climb up left in front of the wall, you reach a plateau of rock. A burial site from the Geometric era (750 BC) was discovered here. A standing stone, similar to a menhir, is visible, above it Apáno Kástro ②.

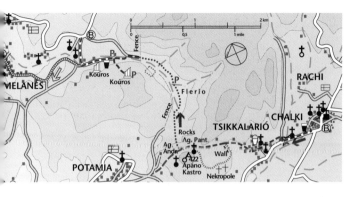

About 30 round or elliptic tombs measuring up to twelve metres in diameter have been excavated. The burial gifts from these dolmens are on display in a raised cabinet in the archaeological museum in Chóra: ceramics, gold jewellery and charred figs and nuts.

0.30 To the right of the wall a path leads up to **Panteleimon chapel** in the saddle. Before that you have to avoid an overgrown section of path by going left. (If you wish to climb up to the Apáno Kástro (see p. 55), go 200 m further until you come to a small doorway on the left in the wall.) Our tour continues right 150 m beyond the chapel and, without a path to the left of the rocks, down into the

★ Flério plateau, which has something mystical about it. Three rocks ③ stand on the edge of the valley, which is green in spring. To the left of the oleander-lined stream, on the slope, it is not difficult to locate tracks with cairns. Cross a sandy dry-bed (**P1**: N 37°04.598'/ E 25°27.770'), then go past a walled field with wind-bent trees at the end

1.00 of the valley on your left. Beside the **dry-bed** you follow the vehicle tracks until these lead up to the right. From there on it is quite strenuous walking at the beginning directly in the dry-bed between oleander bushes. You have

1.15 to open a fence before reaching a **concrete track** (entrance on the right).

When you see a low concrete stele on the left (**P2**: N 37°05.035/ E 25°27.167), go left along the newly laid path for six minutes up through the ancient marble quarry to

1.25 the **Koúros of Farangi**, whose legs broke during transport ④- old photo (**P3**: N 37°04.872'/ E 25°27.232'). Fur-

ther half-carved columns and architectural objects lie
scattered all over the place.

Back in the dry-bed, continue down the concrete track
underneath the trees until several signs point left. Here
1.35   lies the **Koúros of Flério,** the youth in the garden.

> *Koúros statues represent gods or heroes; the female ones
> are called caryatides. This prostrate statue must date
> from the 6th century BC and was presumably intended
> for the Holy Grove in Délos. Due to a flaw in the material
> it was never finished and has remained in this ancient
> quarry ever since.*
>
> *You can buy drinks and small snacks and make yourself
> feel at home in the lovingly tended garden.*

Thus refreshed, you go left along the already familiar concrete track and up right before the car park. Here there is a
new archaeological park, a round-shaped area with a diameter of 40 m. This was the shrine to a goddess of fertility and her two strong sons, the patron saint of stonema-
1.40   sons. The **bus** stops below this *or* on the main road.

> **Alternative:** Those who prefer to catch the bus in
> Melanés proceed through the car park below, up after
> the dry-bed and right round the hill. Soon the village
> can be seen hanging above a terraced valley. On the
> right in the valley are disused water mills. Go up the
1.55   alleys from the lower part of **Mélanes.** Everywhere gi-
> ant cocks' heads advertise the village's popular chick-
2.00   en inns. The **bus** departs in front of one of them,
> *Agkyra.*

⑪ Drosianí, Lady of the Morning Dew

This breathtakingly stunning round-trip leads out of the Tragéa plain along marvellous mule tracks, past the Drosianí church of art-historical importance, up to the mountain village Moní in four to five hours. Orientation is partly hampered by some paths being rather overgrown. Long trousers are therefore suitable. Moní and Chalkí offer good places to stop for refreshment.

■ *9 km, difference in altitude 185 m, moderate*

AWT The bus stops in **Chalkí** (260 m) in front of the large Panagía Protothrónou church, famous for its paintings from seven centuries: the key can be picked up from the pápas, if you are lucky enough to find him. So head down

0.00 the **alley to the right of the kafeníon** and then the second to the right at the Café Citron.

If you walk on ten metres, you run the risk of having to defer your plans: the small platía with the taverna "Yiannis" is a picture-book Greek square.

The second alley right (see above) leads us through the gardens on the edge of the village. We cross a little road and proceed straight on, bearing left (sign "Ag. Diassorí-

0.05 tis") as far as **Marína Chapel** (right) above a cistern. Go down left and then right. (To the left here is a slight, but most worthwhile detour to the very old *Diassorítis Chapel*. It has been completely painted and restored inside with frescoes from the 11th century. Accessible on weekdays until 2.30 pm, see p. 45 ④)

Taking a country lane which traverses the dry-bed, you

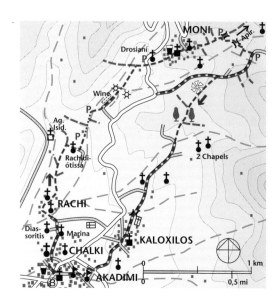

0.10   walk past the chapel (right) in the hamlet **Ráchi** to the far end of the settlement, where you go right and later disregard a double chapel on the left. Go right at the ruin at the exit from the hamlet. You now proceed along one of

★   the most beautiful Cycladic trails ①, keeping parallel with the counterslope. Our half-way point, Moní, is visible above right in the hills. At the fork you turn down left to the oakwood, at the next one up right on a paved trail. To your left, on the counterslope, the ruins of the Isidorios church with three naves comes into view. When you have

0.20   almost drawn **level with** the church, climb up a steep, naturally stepped path on the right to the superbly situated, but closed **Rachidiótissa Church** ② (**P2:** N 37° 04.395'/ E 25°29.069'). It contains frescoes from the 14th century.

Now continue across the hill, then downhill and left after 20 m. A slightly overgrown monopáti leads gently down-

0.25   hill through large olive groves into a **dry-bed** and on above the left side of the stream. Shortly afterwards you change sides and the stream is now on your left. Press on through the "stream" between oleander bushes and man-size dragon arum, which lures insects with the odour of rotten meat. Further ahead are paths leading uphill both on the right and on the left. The shady **defile** (**P2:** N 37°04.586'/ E 25°29.188') ascending *diagonally* to the right leads us on to a broad lane, where you proceed straight ahead. On the left are cisterns in a fenced-off vineyard. At the end of the fence we stalk about 100 m straight on across a field into a transverse dry-bed (do not go up right to the water mill). Along a wall-lined path you then come to two paled gates (left). There on the right a

0.45 **splendid monopáti** leads up the hill. Skip across the road at the top (**P3:** N 37°04.871'/ E 25°29.582') on to a wonderful, wide **paved track** and immediately left to the clock-tower in the olive grove!

0.50 *The **Panagía Drosianí**, "Our Lady of the Morning Dew", is, despite its name, the oldest church on the island. The chancel with the three apses from the 4th century BC is the oldest part. In the 7th century two cavernous oratories were added next to it, then in the 12th century both sections were connected with one another by the large rectangular main room.*

The frescoes are famous; in the main cupola the oldest layers are as much as 1400 years old and thus the oldest in the Balkans. This church is open!

0.55 Then you stroll on along the kalderími up to the **perimeter of Moní.** If you do not intend to stop at the nice panoramic inn "Panorama" (445 m, above the church), amble on up through the gently rising village, which otherwise has little to recommend it. At the far end, go down

1.00 between **two chapels** ③ to the old washing troughs just beyond the village, from where a small concrete path leads up to terraced gardens. At a fork drop down to the

	right and, after a hollow, climb up again. On the way up
1.10	you come to a new small **concrete bridge** (**P4:** N 37°04.945'/ E 25°30.193'), where the staircase to Apíranthos begins.
!!	But *before that* we go down the marble steps on the right and, after another bridge, right up through the dry-bed. On the other side, on the same level as Moní, we proceed round bends and over even, though sunken, ground.
1.25	Walking past a path-crossing, we come to a **country lane** (**P5:** N 37°04.644'/ E 25°29.883'), which we stride down to the right. We ignore two monopátia branching off left. 70
!!	m after a roadway has joined from the right a two-metre
1.30	wide **monopáti** forks *left in a right-hand bend*. We do so too!

Over on the hill to the right are two windmill torsos. We head downhill between some rocks, ahead of us the Tragéa plain with its villages and, towering above them, the three Venetian fortress-house towers and the dome of the church of Kalóxylos. Up here are ***resting places with a view over Mount Zás.

There is no getting lost on the way down. The dome of Kalóxylos is our goal. Two rural chapels lie picturesquely among the olive trees on the left ④. Below, shortly before

| 1.40 | the **dry-bed** (rocky ledges), begins a roadway through the olive groves. Descend to the right when it forks. Along the wayside are a few deserted houses and washing troughs (left), a bridge and a graveyard. Soon we are standing in |
| 1.50 | front of the closed Triáda church of **Kalóxylos.** And nobody knows where the pápas is. |

| | From here we march left, down to the road, and are guid- |
| 2.00 | ed slightly left to **Chalkí** by the Venetian Gratsía tower. If you are unlucky, you may end up at the Politís tower in Akádimi, a neighbouring village. In which case you will need a few minutes more. Perhaps there is still time for a glass at "Yiannis" (**P6:** N 37°03.749'/ E 25°28.936'). |

⑫ Two churches in the olive grove

The description offers two options:
A) a two-hour tour from Chalkí to Filóti;
B) a circular hike round Chalkí.
Following paths and country lanes, you pass two important Byzantine churches and a Venetian tower-house and stroll through numerous olive groves. For somewhere to take a break you have to wait until you get back, half way along spring water is available free of charge.
■ *A) 4 km, altitude difference 140 m, easy-moderate*
■ *B) 5 km, altitude difference 90 m, easy*

AWT 0.00	From the bus stop in **Chalkí**, proceed 150 m down the street and, already before the bridge, left at the left turn down to the washing area. Opposite this you ascend and go left immediately, then after one minute right at a fork
0.05	until you come to a **concrete track**. Here you go left, straightaway passing under a large oak tree and left at a fork. At the branch to the left (with signpost) you walk straight ahead on gravel until you see, raised up on the left, the old Byzantine church with its cross-vaulted dome
0.15	**Ayíi Apóstoli Metochíou** ①.

The façade is adorned with exceptionally sophisticated blind arches. The dome of the painted, unusually tall church rests on four piers. The remains of wall paintings from the 12th and 13th centuries are preserved. It is open on weekdays from 10.00 am to 2.30 pm – if you are lucky.

Continue in the same direction through the hamlet **Metóchi** to the main road. On the far side, diagonally on

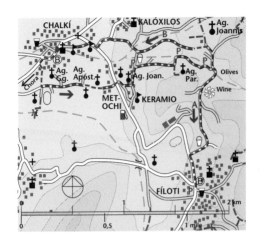

the right, climb up past a church (left) and through
Keramí, later bearing left to the medieval Venetian tower-
house, **Pýrgos Kalavrós**. Saunter down the paved alley
between the houses.

0.20

> *At the end of the village, on the left, stands the important
> Byzantine church Ayos Ioánnis Pródromos. It contains
> superb frescoes. Four angels surround the pantokrátor, the
> universal ruler. With a little diplomatic skill you can ob-
> tain the key in the neighbouring house.*

0.25 If you do not use the **spring** which follows (**P1:**
N37°03.739'/ E25°29.473'), turn off up to the right already 40 m earlier and gradually walk uphill along a concrete track, later under trees near the stream. Shortly after
the concrete surfacing ends and the old paving stones

0.30   reappear, the path **forks.** (Going right will bring you to Paraskeví chapel.) We go left (B2) and later ignore the inviting natural steps to the right, rather walking down-

0.35   hill, partly across modern sand-lime brick, to the **dry-bed** (**P2:** N37°03.772'/ E25°29.795', 330 m). We climb up the dry-bed for one minute (or 120 metres) as far as a path which takes us on up to the right. At a garden gate we drop to the left and back into the dry-bed (**P3:** N37°03.705'/ E25°29.985'). After a few metres a left turn

0.45   takes us up to a **roadway.**

       Here **Tour B** goes left (see below).

       Ramble up the roadway to the right and, after 200 m, over a dry-bed to the right. On the left vines grow on the now

0.50   concreted path. Below a windmill (left) you cross a **small hill** (400 m) and see Filóti spread out before you. At the fork you naturally take the easier option, in other words the one leading downhill. Where the path joins a larger street, you drop to the right at a well, and again at the next fork. And on the main street you make for the street

1.05   cafés of **Filóti** up on the left as fast as your legs can carry you! Hungry hikers can expect a satisfying portion in Nicolas' taverna, across the street not much more than coffee ③ (**P4:** N37°03.117'/ E25°29.870', 355 m).

Tour B:

0.45   On the **roadway** you walk left, likewise at the second fork, and turn, in front of a house (left) – even before St. John's chapel ④ – down left into a sunken path. On the right we are soon greeted by the large dome of Kalóxilos church, before we reach the main road after a left-hand bend. There we turn down right, after 80 m diagonally left in to a little side road and saunter past a big Venetian

1.00   tower-house to **Chalkí.**

The World of the Gods

At the beginning of all things, the Terra Mater, Gaia, the goddess of the earth, appeared out of Chaos. In her sleep, she bore Uranos out of herself and took him as her husband.

Kronos and his sister Rhea, as well as other Titans, resulted from this unusual relationship. The two of them also united, upholding the family's tradition, and parented the goddesses Hera (later the Roman Juno, protector of the military aristocracy), Hertia (the Roman Vesta, goddess of the domestic hearth) and Demeter (Ceres, goddess of the fields) as well as the gods Zeus (Jupiter), Poseidon (Neptune) and Hades (Pluto).

The men divided up the world among themselves: Zeus took Olympus and thus domination; his brothers had the sea and the underworld. Zeus, the highest of the gods, lord of heaven and earth, is said to have spent his youth in a cave on Náxos ⑬, brought up by an eagle. He also took his sister Demeter as his wife, who bore the gods Ares (Mars, the Roman god of war), Eilythia, Hebe and Hephaistos (Vulcan). From Zeus's relationships with 15 other godly sisters, there resulted, among others, Artemis, Apollo, Hermes and Aphrodite. Artemis (Roman Diana) is the goddess of the hunt; Apollo represents right, order and peace; Hermes (Mercury) is the protector of wanderers, shepherds, tradesmen and rogues, while Aphrodite (Venus) is the goddess of sensual love and beauty.

Zeus did not just have his way in heaven. Meanwhile, there were lovely princesses on earth, too. He approached them in various forms, for example as a bull, swan and even as the husband of one of the women he desired. Thus the Heroes Minos, Perseus, Helena and Herakles, in addition to fifteen others, were born. They were, however, only half-gods, representing the link between heaven and earth. Semele, the mortal king's daughter from Thebes, bore him the god Dionysos (Roman Bacchus), according to legend in the Jénnesis cave (birthplace) near Engáres on Náxos ⑳. He was the god of wine and fertility. Dionysos gave Náxos the wine, at that time considered the best in Greece. In his second capacity he took care of Ariadne, who had been left behind by Theseus on the beach on Náxos when he returned after killing the Minotaur in Crete. Through the liaison Ariadne rose to become a (demi-) goddess, while the unfaithful Theseus plunged his father Aigéus into disaster, i.e. the sea. The name "Aegean" is just about the only tangible fact to have remained from the era of the gods.

⑬ Good Zeus!

Today we're going alpine – by tackling the steep western side of Zeus, the highest mountain in the Cyclades! Besides protection against the sun and wind, and a bottle of water, a torch may also come in very handy for the Zeus cave. Although a head for heights is not required for the four-hour mountain tour, orientation skills are important, for we follow not just old paved tracks but cross-country trails too.

■ *8 km, difference in altitude 650 m, difficult*

▷ *Map see p. 71*

▷ Map see p. 71

AWT 0.00	At the bus stop in **Filóti** (345 m) you should first choose a taverna for the way back and then head off along the gently climbing main street in the direction of Apíranthos. About 300 m after the second bus stop take the road on the right beside the mini-chapel, towards Chimárrou.
0.10	*Alternative:* 300 m after this chapel you find on the left a **well-beaten track** up to the dominating white cruciform-domed church of Agía Iríni built in 1995. If you do not wish to use the path described below, whose first stretch has been burnt off in 2006, you can go right on the small road beyond the church, round the hill and slowly uphill to the car park as well (**P1:** N 37°02.204'/ E 25°29.625').

Otherwise you follow the road at the bottom as far as a fork on the right to an industrial building. *60 m before that* you veer diagonally up to the left on rocky slabs and

0.15   on to a **path.** It later becomes visible, then almost at once skirts a windmill (left) and is transformed into a wonderful mule track which leads left uphill. Just a pity that wedding fireworks set fire to some of the trees in the summer of 2006. The scorch marks end after 10 minutes.

0.25   At the **fork** in front of a walled field with gate you wander left up through the second gate on to the left of this one.

0.30   After going through further gates you see **house ruins** below on the right. From there you proceed for a short stretch below a subsided path, later describe a left arc past houses (left) until you see the steep Mount Zeus ①. Above retaining walls is the car park and beyond that a shady

0.40   place to rest with a **well** (**P1:** N 37°02.204'/ E 25°29.625', 510m). Your bottle of water replenished, the climb can now commence.

      A recently laid paved path forms the first part, later a steep track leads up through the rocks, past another well,

0.55   to the roughly 100 m deep **Cave of Zeus** ②. (**P2:** N 37°02.076'/ E 25°29.987', 630 m) Here he is said to have spent his first years as a God, but this is claimed of quite a number of caves. Without a torch that must have been an inhospitable childhood. Inside the cave, to the right, are quite sizeable rooms which one tends to overlook at first. In the gorge one gazes up at the precipitous mountain in disbelief ③. But, no fear, up there on the left we will be hiking on perfectly safe tracks. The stony path first leads on up through the gorge and then turns left out of the

1.05   gorge below a **field of scree** and runs steeply uphill as far

1.10   as a **fence**, parallel with a wall (**P3:** N 37°02.118'/ E 25°30.076', 740 m). The magnificent view compensates for the strenuous ascent.

Follow the fence up to the right. When the fence turns to the left near some rocks walk straight on. Below a field of scree climb up to the left in the direction of one or two man-size stone towers. Heading for the cairns, gain height

1.30 and climb straight up to the **stone towers** (905 m)! There you spot the peak on the right and the well-beaten paths leading thither.

1.40 A concrete block marks the **summit of Zás** (also Za or Zefs); we have reached the highest point on the Cyclades, 1001 metres above the harbour of Náxos town and more than 600 m above Filóti. The people appear to have great respect for Zeus: here there is neither a chapel nor an antenna to disturb the majesty of the mightiest of the Greek Gods (p. 67). After refreshing our knowledge of island place-names we drink to his health (**P4:** N 37°01.818'/ E 25° 30.138').

To return to Filóti you take the same path for 200 m, then swing right towards the Bay of Apóllonas and follow the path marked "2". A more frequented trail, it runs downhill to the right of the top of a foothill. Later you swing

2.10 left in the direction of Filóti and come to the round **lime kilns** (**P5:** N 37°02.294'/ E 25°30.777', 745 m), later still past a well. The marvellous paved path ④ ends at the

2.35 chapel **Ayía Marína** (**P6:** N 37°02.545'/ E 25°30.493').

Now turn into the road on the left and elegantly shorten

2.50 the serpentine bends in order to get down to the **main road.** Go along this to the left for about 50 m and then, thirsty, descend the staircase, later crossing a car park, to

3.10 **Filóti**, where those nice landlords are already waiting to receive us.

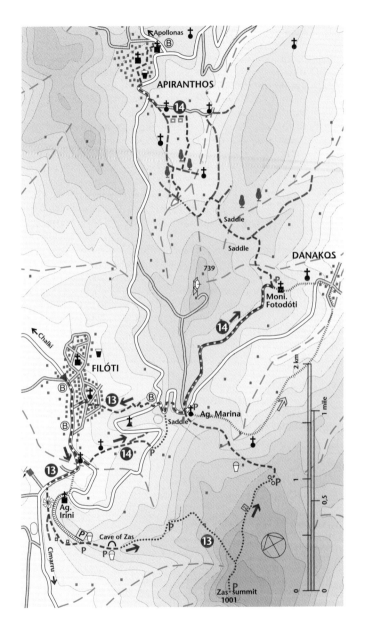

⑭ The mysterious monastery

The glorious, three to four-hour hike begins in Filóti,
leads to a deserted monastery and then along mule
tracks through rolling countryside to the pretty
mountain village of Apíranthos. This is the first
place with somewhere to stop and a well. The bus
returns from there at about 4.15 pm.
■ *9 km, difference in altitude 270 m, moderate*

▷ *Map see previous page*

AWT **Short cut:** Do not leave the bus until the turn-off (Greek diakladosi) for Danakós/Zas, from where it takes eight minutes on the road to the chapel Ayía Marína (p. 79).

0.00 From **Filóti bus station** head 700 m along the road to the end of the village (or alight at the second stop in Filóti). After a rough stone wall (left), before the beginning of a

0.07 wide curve right, follow a **monopáti** going left up the slope, along whose upward incline you soon come across a chapel. Keeping right later on at the fork, continue on

0.20 up to the **road** (**P1**: N 37°02.684'/ E 25°30.207'). Right opposite you see a few markers indicating a scarcely identifiable track. Bear uphill and left in the direction of the trees in the saddle, which lies to the right below a

0.35 summit chapel. In this **saddle** you go to the right of the wall enclosure to the road and from there 80 m to the right up a short cut leading back to the road and on along

0.40 it to the **Chapel Ayía Marína** ①. (**P2**: N 37°02.545'/ E 25°30.493')

Alternative: On the left beside the chapel a mule track runs down into the pretty village of **Danakós**, where you can stop for a rest and then proceed along a beautiful kalderími up to Fotodóti.

At the chapel we turn off the road to the left and take the level dirt track straight ahead to Fotodóti. With a spring in our step we wander along above terraces, gardens and groves, beneath oak and olive trees, until we imagine we see a Venetian fortress-house tower ②. But it is supposed

1.00 to be a fortress-like **monastery** (**P3**: N 37°03.032'/ E 25° 31.270').

> *The enchantingly situated **Moní Christóu Fotodóti** (light-bringing Christ) turns out to be a 12–13 m high rampart. Inside a church has been integrated half way up. Above this the curtain wall is hollow, the former timber floors have disappeared.*
>
> *The building's history remains a mystery. It is assumed that an early Christian church was heightened with lateral ramparts in the 16th century and expanded into a branch monastery of the St. John's monastery in Pátmos.*

Back on our previous path, we turn right and continue above a private dwelling and below a vineyard on a quiet track leading to the opposite slope. Going straight ahead

!! in the gap, we then follow the track along the slope *to the*
1.10 *right* up to the **saddle**. There is a gate here and another *di-*
!! *rectly opposite*, barely visible in a fence (**P4:** N37°03.251'/ E25°31.255', 660 m). Then we see Apíranthos on the other side of the valley.

★ Strolling along a monopáti above a plateau ③, it is a plea-
1.25 sure to proceed to a second **saddle** via the wide valley. The continuation of this track is in the direction of the

previous path, on the right beside a wall. Later you descend to the left in zigzags to a fork. From there *left* downhill, through a ditch and up the other side. Keeping to a stony path, and later without a path, but bearing left, you

1.35 soon come to a small **retaining weir** on the next valley floor. In spring this can be a little difficult to negotiate. On the far side you follow a sunken path, but go up to the

1.40 right after 30 m. Beside an **oak** you drop to the right and then up again left to the next oak ④ and straight ahead. Paths lead uphill beside the cattle troughs, eventually leading to a roadway. In **Apíranthos** you have to find your way through some confusing marble steps, but then

2.00 you can chill out on the **platía**, one of the finest on these islands, or at "Leftéris" with grand views over the valley. It is another five minutes to the bus.

ISBN 978-3-9808802-7-5

⑮ A lonely tower

This hike on footpaths along the eastern side of Mt. Zás lasts six to seven hours. In Filóti it is possible to call a taxi at 6977939321 (or 22850-31712) which will take you the 15 km to the start at the Chimárrou tower for about eleven euro. The paths on this impressive walk through the isolated rocky mountainous scenery are mostly unmarked – certain tracking skills are therefore required. The only (possibly) clear water is to be found at the very end.
■ *11 km, difference in altitude 390 m, difficult*

AWT Once the taxi driver Jakobos has delivered us to **Chimárrou tower** ①, the first thing we do is to take a closer look at this monument:

> *The imposing Hellenic round tower consists of dry white marble blocks in two shells with a thickness of one metre and is roughly 2300 years old. As a fortifiable farmstead, it was originally four metres higher and had several timber floors inside. The only window is above the entrance, serving a defensive purpose with stones and boiling oil. Surrounding the tower were houses protected by a wall. An Early Christian basilica was found beneath the two chapels.*

0.00 From the **tower** we go 300 m back along the road. After a
0.10 right turn-off, and after the **bridge**, we pass through two openings in the fence on the right and descend, balancing on boulders. On the left beside the waist-high stone wall, which runs diagonally to the left into the valley
0.15 floor, we find trails which, after the **dry-bed**, continue to

the right of the wall running uphill ②. Where this wall swings left further up, we proceed without a path in the direction we have been going and on

0.35 into the **saddle** (**P1**: N 37°00.440'/ E 25°31. 020', 495 m).

From here it is possible to behold the broad back of Mount Zeus and beneath it, about 3 km away, a half-hidden house, our first destination. Running along the hillside in front is a brown roadway; beneath it, just above a fairly long row of rocks, runs the path we will later be taking ③.

From the saddle we walk beside the rocks on the left, then down to the right through a hollow to the said row of rocks, beneath which a solitary olive tree survives. Indistinct tracks lead across the foothills of the mountain. On the far side is a valley, where it is possible to discern an alternative path, which subsequently turns off our route.

However we do not take this, but stay at the same height to save our strength – life is hard enough as it is. But the downside is that our track is more difficult to find. Keeping on the level, continue as far as the wooded end of the valley and then up along the fence to the farm. While doing so, we take the opportunity to recall the names of the various Small Cyclades dotted about in the sea – in case of doubt referring to the inside cover of our guide-book.

Immediately behind the farmhouse

1.15 **Fountana** (550 m) is a gate, which lets us go up to the roadway. Through a wide gate in the fence we come to a

1.30 fork and go right to **St. John's Chapel** (**P2**: N37°01.357'/ E25°30.885', 580 m).

Before it we descend right, further down at the fork left as far as a left turn beside a skeleton tree at the waterhole – before the farmstead. A roadway leads us down into the green valley floor. There we wander alongside the wall (right) until reaching the ascent between two tall walls. Later we climb up without a path between round bushes and, at the top, on alongside the wall on the right. This

2.10 will guide us for a while yet, finally ending at a **cluster of trees** ④. Just behind that we proceed to the right of a wall

2.20 **through** a wooded hollow and then up to the highest point of our trek at 745 metres above sea level.

Almost simultaneously the panorama across Apíranthos opens up. The wall on the left ends soon afterwards – this is where the ascent to Mt. Zeus branches off. We go straight ahead, later down a pleasant paved path. On the right in the valley lies the village Danakós, above it the

2.45 castlelike monastery Fotodótis ⑭. Soon we reach **Ayía Marína** chapel (**P3:** N 37°02.671′/ E 25°30.435′, 585 m), where we can donate a candle out of gratitude.

Continue left along the road and then, taking a short cut

2.55 to the left of the guardrail, down to the **main road** Filóti-Apíranthos. The bus to Náxos town passes here at around 4.25 pm. The footpath to Filóti is described on page 70.

⑯ The source in Danakós

The five-hour tour leads down into the valley of Danakós and back up again along old marble steps to the restored monastery Fotodótis. Here the hike could be shortened by one hour. Both alternatives end in Filóti.
Path-finding skills are useful in a number of places. Danakós not only has the source to offer, but a nice little taverna as well.

■ *7 km, difference in altitude 2 x 200 m, moderate or difficult*

AWT 0.00	Leave the bus behind Filóti at the **stop "Ayía Marína"** (also "Zás" or "Zefs") and go 50 m up the road that branches off. Here a well-beaten path provides a short cut to the right, but later returns to the road. Go up it shortly until you find another short cut to the right. A level section of
0.10	road later leads to the **Ayía Marína** chapel (**P1**: N 37°02.545'/ E 25°30.493', 610 m)
0.25	20 m to the left of the chapel you find a shady path dropping down into the valley ①, on the left side of which lies a heavily overgrown hollow. Having traversed a **streamlet** (**P2**: N 37°02.551'/ E 25°30.724') you look down into a gorge on the left. This is where orientation becomes difficult: 50 m further on you pass through a gap *in a wall* and come to a luscious meadow. After another 60 m you reach
!!	a *little wall* ②. Climb over it *on the right-hand side* and bear right up small trails (with water pipes) which lead in to a passage between green bushes and yellow gorse (right). Walking to the left of the gorse, you find a more distinct

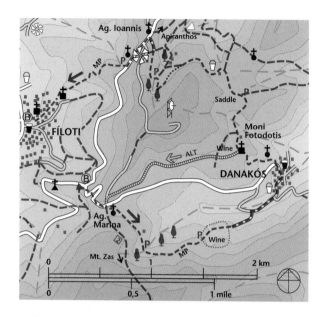

path to the right of a fence with brambles, which tend to
!!   give ramblers a hard time. Thereafter you turn *down left*
on rock slabs and then immediately right between the
trees.

At the following clearing you walk straight ahead and
0.30   through a **little gate** (**P3:** N 37°02.589′/ E 25°30.910′) into a vineyard. After descending through this, you leave it
again through another tiny gate.

0.35   From here a **roadway** leads in to the valley and to a fairly
wide sand road, which you follow to the right. Shortly before the village, at the end of the retaining wall on the
0.50   left, steps lead down left to **Danakós source** (410 m) ③. A
giant plane shades the idyllic village square and one has
to repress the desire to lie down in the crystal-clear water!
Downstream are the ruins of mills fed by water from up-
stream.

Steps and alleys bring you up through the village to the
little taverna *Florakas*. Opposite it concrete steps show the
way ahead. Further up you cross the road 20 m diagonally
to the right to marble steps, which are more pleasing to
walk on. A wide paved path, a kalderími overlooking the

1.15	island of Donoússa, leads up to the **Fotodótis monastery** 4 (p. 73).

> ***Short cut:*** The way described below necessitates clambering over walls and coping with a greater difference in altitude. From the monastery it is more comfortable to take the country lane on the left at the next fork

(1.35) and return to the **Ayía Marína chapel**. There one goes right and then follows the description on page 70

(2.10) as far as **Filóti!**

The longer way leads from Fotodótis monastery to the same fork but there to the right, on above a holiday house

!! (right), into a transverse stream and behind that up *right* on a very beautiful path 5 alongside a fence (right). As a

1.25 sunken path it leads to **two gates** (**P4:** N 37°03.251'/ E 25°31.255', 660 m), which come one after another at a distance of only a few metres.

> ***Alternative:*** In ⑭, AWT 1.10, is a description of the trail which runs from here to **Apíranthos.**

Behind the second gate you go to the left and, for quite a while, on the right side of a wall. Twice you have to avoid overgrown sections by keeping right, always enjoying a fabulous view over Apíranthos. On the polished slabs in the saddle which follows you must search for the rather

!! hidden sunken path *on the left.* It leads to a source in an open, green area.

From here you go up to the right beside the fence until

1.35 where a **mule track** begins. This goes right in the direction of St. John's church with the offset roof. In a left curve

!! it runs along the slope towards terraced fields. *Before it descends, climb over* the walls running at right angles to the valley and cross, on the same level, the terraces spread

out below the aerial on the hill. In the wooded dip before the next opposite slope you find a path, which you go
2.00 down right until you come to **brick steps** (**P5:** N 37°03.359'/ E 25°30.722'). Here a mule track ascends left,
2.05 passing through several gates  before reaching the **road** and ending at Ayios Ioánnis church (620 m) on the steep hillside. This is where you may wish to stop the bus at around 4.20 pm.

But if you go left 100 m down the road, you discover another small chapel on the right. Proceeding even further along the road, you see a mule track in front of a fence on the right, below the guardrail (**P6:** N 37°03.419'/ E 25°30.569'). Initially it descends alongside the power poles. From the saddle you then get a view of Filóti, which
2.30 you later reach to the right of the **church** on the knoll. You take a few paces to the right above a flat roof, down steps and past the large church (right) to the bus stop in
2.35 **Filóti** on the road. You can unwind again after the strenuous hike in one of the shady cafés. The bus from Apóllonas comes at 4.30 pm.

⑰ Up Mount Fanári

This very beautiful four to five-hour hike goes up Fanári, the third highest mountain on Náxos, with a short climb. From there it continues down an old stepped trail in to the fertile Tragéa plain. One then roams through olive groves on the upper edge of the plain before coming to Chalkí, where one can take the bus back after a well-earned rest. In spring streams afford a chance to draw water.

■ *9 km, difference in altitude 580 m, moderate to difficult*

AWT	By bus it takes one hour to reach **Apíranthos** (570 m).
0.00	From the last bus stop at the memorial you go to the right of the large Church of the Assumption to enter the little town and stroll past several cafés with views of the valley. At the kafeneio "Apíranthos" you come to the platía, which spreads out to the right.
	There you proceed to the right of the seven long steps through a passage and up steps, downhill again for a bit, then left and straight up. At the top down six steps and then immediately up right: On the right-hand side stands
0.08	the **Ayía Paraskeví church** ①.
	Above the church you walk 100 m on along the concrete road and then turn off left into a little road. This rises
0.12	steeply and 30 m beyond a tall cistern you head up a **path** on the left. You're now on the trail!
	The path soon passes through a gate leading in to pasture
!!	land; *50 m beyond it you follow the serpentines up to the*
0.20	*right.* After another **gate** begins a wonderful, wall-lined

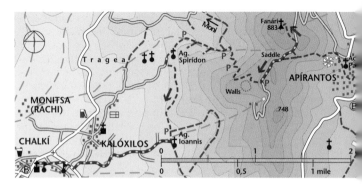

★   monopáti, which later hugs the slope as a stepped trail.

0.30   Turning right later on, you come to a **saddle** on a roadway (**P1:** N 37°04.464'/ E 25°30.784') and march up to the right for two minutes. At a transverse wall on a small sad-

0.40   dle you turn up left and arrive at the **summit of Mount Fanári** ② (883 m). Apart from the visually unsuccessful chapel there is nothing to impair the distant view. Lying at your feet is the Tragéa plain with Chalkí. To the north you can make out the stepped trail for the way down, which from here looks steeper than it is.

Returning the same way, you are soon back in the wide

0.50   **saddle** and walk along the roadway on the next hill until

0.55   a **left bend.** On the right below there are enclosed pastures ③. At this point (**P2:** N 37°04.264'/ E 25°30.567') you turn off down to the right, continuing outside the walls. A little further down you turn off right and find a skilfully built stepped trail into the valley ④.

You saunter downhill in elegant wide curves. Further

1.20 down you then have to pay more attention to the little red dots again, which lead in front of a transverse **field wall** (**P3:** N 37°04.367'/ E 25°30.378').

Here you go right and, after a dip, proceed in a dry-bed covered with oleander. On smoothly polished rock you then reach another wall (**P4:** N 37°04.436'/ E 25°30.301'). The arrows point to the right.

But not for us, we don't want to go to Moní. We go left and cross the smooth rock to reach the far side of the stream after another 10 m and finding a path leading downhill. After two minutes it leads straight into the dry-bed, where you go through a gate. Now stay in or on the left of the stream for about 20 minutes, first passing an

1.30 overgrown **cattle-trough.** Ignore two paths to the left.

1.35 Below a clump of trees you see a **small cistern** on the

1.40 right. Further down the stream is fenced off above a **waterfall** (**P5:** N 37°04.502'/ E 25°30.030').

From here a shady mule track runs left, down past the picturesquely situated chapel Ayios Spiridon, through a gate

1.45 and, sunken, to a **roadway.**

Take this 80 m down to the left, where a dream path continues on up left. (Soon after it can be necessary to overcome a few wooden obstacles.) You now promenade beneath oaks, later in an olive grove, above the abundantly irrigated and fertile plain of Tragéa, which is dotted with tens of thousands of olive trees. Clinging to the hillside above is the village Moní.

2.05 Our panorama path ends at a **country lane** (**P6:** N 37°03.939'/ E 25°29.909'). Up left is the St. John's chapel. Although closed, it affords us a wonderful place to rest.

We descend the roadway to the right, straight on at the right junction and down right in to a sunken path at the

2.15 **fork.** The large dome of Kalóxilos church greets us on the right before we reach the main road after a left-hand bend. There we turn down right, bearing left after 80 m in to a little side street and past a Venetian residence tower

2.25 towards **Chalkí.**

⑱ Unusual frescoes

This very enjoyable five-hour round-trip on old stone paths and country lanes shows the variety of land-scapes which Náxos has to offer. Although partly shaded, it has no spring with water. Along the route is an age-old chapel, which houses unusual frescoes. However, the bus timetable only allows less than six hours for the hike!

■ *14 km, difference in altitude 100 m, moderate to difficult*

AWT
0.00

From the **upper bus stop in Apíranthos** at the war memorial (590 m) you enter the town across the street, then immediately turn down right and under the road bridge. The stone path divides 30 m beyond that – we head down to the left (...and will return, tired and thirsty, along the upper path). After eight minutes you reach a country lane, which you follow 200 m down to some

0.10

steps, which lead left.

Short cut: One could stay on the more convenient, but not so beautiful lane until AWT 0.37.

After the steps a wall-lined mule track runs past a chapel (right) in to a dry-bed and then on to the right. Several gates now have to be negotiated. It is a pleasure to stroll between the fields and gardens of the farmers ①. Having

0.15

found a **wider path** (**P1:** N37°04.598'/ E 25°31.285'), you go left a few paces until you find elegant steps leading up-hill on the right.

Later you turn down right a few paces in front of a tallish

0.25

wall – the stone covering was washed away here – and

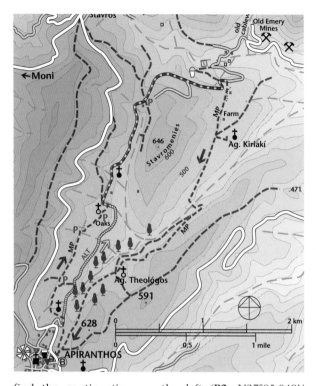

find the continuation on the left (**P2:** N37°05.048'/ E25°31.524', 500 m). While the path is overgrown with grass from here on, it can be easily identified by means of

0.30   the tall wall and fence on the left. It leads through **oak**
0.35   **trees** to the picturesque ruins of a **double chapel** ② (**P3:** N37°05.205'/ E25°31.639'). Remains of the interior painting are preserved.

Then proceed down across a dry-bed and, after two minutes, to a country lane – the short cut described above. Here you climb left, come through a gully just before a

0.45   farmhouse (right) and go round **two bends** below the ruins of a house.

1.00   Walking straight ahead along the lane, you come to a **saddle** (**P4:** N37°05.838'/ E25°32.000'). Here begins an excessively wide track, subsidized landscape degradation. To recover from the shock, let your eyes wander across the sea:

to Donoússa and Amorgós. On the opposite slope is the cavernous emery mine, which was closed down in 1989 when it became unprofitable. A material ropeway used to extend down to the harbour in Moutsóuna (see p. 103).

Below the first sharp left-hand bend of the track you later see the old path marked "1" which, miraculously, has almost survived unscathed. Cutting off the next bend, you find an entrance on the right beside the track and, on the right beside this, raised a little, the old paved path which was intact up until 2007. It is a godsend to stumble across such a rural idyll. Above the fields on the left, barely perceptible, stands a brown chapel on the hill ③ – our destination. After a second gate a wooden sign points us to the

1.30 left through a farmstead to **Kyriakí Church.**

Its interior houses a rarity: The wall painting from the iconoclasm, the iconoclastic controversy in the 8th and 9th centuries. In those days the ideas of Islam also influenced Christianity, including that prohibiting the pictorial representation of God. During the hundred-year controversy church paintings emerged with geometric and floral motifs (see p.17). That explains why animals (birds and fishes) are depicted here in the apse.

Back on the main route, you continue left almost on the
1.45 same level ③, then downhill and over a **bridge** (395 m), before ascending again. On the right in the green valley you hear the tinkling of tiny goat-bells, while you plod on up – by now rather parched – beneath shady kermes oaks.
2.15 You therefore disregard the **branch-off** to the left, which would bring you to the closed-off ruins of Theológos church in four minutes, and soon arrive at the bus stop in
2.35 **Apíranthos.**

⑲ The long way to Chalkí

This four to five-hour hike runs through a little known region to Moní and, past the famous Byzantine chapels of the Tragéa plain, to Chalkí. At first it follows a roadway, then without a path at all for quite a stretch, later on mule tracks. Path-finding skills are useful in the middle section, long trousers are recommended in many parts. There are places to stop off in Moní and Chalkí.

■ *11 km, difference in altitude 320 m, moderate*

AWT 0.00	Having alighted from the bus at the **Stávros-Keramotí chapel** (between Apíranthos and Kóronos), you go down the side-street directly opposite the chapel door (not the level street to Moní!). After eight minutes you leave it in the second sharp right-hand bend and turn left in to a sand road. Descending slightly, this circles the valley between vineyards, offering a view of the village Keramotí
0.20	(B1). In a saddle lies the hamlet **Kadís** (p. 93 ①), where it is possible to draw water.
!!	50 m after the marble table, after a spring (left), you turn *left* off the roadway and ascend a narrow, yet identifiable trail ②. It runs between olive trees and, soon afterwards,
0.25	through a **gully**, after which a wall-lined monopáti begins. It is not long before the accompanying walls disappear again and you walk alongside the retaining wall on the right-hand side. Orientation becomes more difficult – your destination is the saddle straight ahead and slightly to the right. Coming over from the right you hear the dull thuds from the detonations in the nearby marble quarries.

0.40 Soon you reach the **saddle** (590 m), with a low goat-pen. If you look straight ahead and see the boldly erected Barbara chapel on the peak, you know you are right.

A little further down are two withered olive trees in your direction of movement; there – a little to the left – further tracks lead down through the phrýgana. Later, on the right side of the path, comes a

0.50 larger **goat-pen**.

Traverse the deeper, wide hollow (515 m) ③, watching out for the filed off mountains of Kinídaros on the right, the largest marble quarries on Náxos. In front of you are walls, on the left-hand side of which you hunt down a transverse,

0.55 sunken **monopáti** (P1: N 37° 05.736'/ E 25°30.162'). Going left along it, you turn right at the turn-off after just 10 m and then descend a shady and beautiful trail! ④

At the bottom you walk left for

1.05 about 30 m along the **dry-bed** between the gardens, then uphill right along a country lane – soon using the Barbara chapel as a lighthouse. On the following road you turn first right, then left at the junction and, overlooking the Tragéa plain and Mount Zás, pro-

1.25 ceed into **Moní** (460 m).

In the restaurant *Panorama* (right) you could initially make the most of your stay or alternatively, just 50 m beyond it, turn off right. Steps lead downhill and, after a right-hand bend, more lead out of the village. The paved path affords a view of the dome of a chapel down on the right. At a fork you go right

and soon you are standing in front of the oldest church
1.35 on Náxos, **Panagía Drosianí**, to the right of the path
(see p. 61).

Further down you cross the road and enter a marvellous,
shady mule track, which leads downhill and then left.
Later you traverse a little stream. On the right-hand edge
1.45 of a fenced vineyard is an old **water mill.**

Near the entrance gate to the vineyard you leave the lane,
go down a few steps and – at the fork – *straight ahead* into
1.50 a narrow path. This later leads into the **dry-bed (P2:**
37°04,586′/ E25°29,188′), which you leave again after
four minutes at rock slabs, going up right. There you find
a rather overgrown mule track, which runs to the right of
and above the stream. Raised up on the right the ancient
Rachidiótissa chapel (P3: N37°04,395′/ E25°29,069′,
p. 59 ②) soon comes into view. It houses old frescoes, but
is unfortunately closed.

Passing it, you descend the old natural steps on the left
and, further down at the fork, left. On the opposite slope
stands the deserted Isidóros church with three naves.
★ Spread out behind giant oaks on the wayside is a stupen-
dous landscape. Turning left at a fork, and right at the
2.10 next after the steps, you arrive in **Ráchi.**

There you go left, through the village and beyond it cross
the dry-bed. You turn off right at once from the following
concrete track (at the sign Ayios Georgios Diasoritis) into
a path, later left. (Heading right would bring you to the
early Byzantine Diasorítis chapel, see p. 45).) On the left
by the wayside comes a chapel above a spring, before you
2.20 reach your goal for the day: **Chalkí (P4:** N 37°03.749′/ E
25°28.936′, 270 m).

⑳ The marble mountains of Kinídaros

This downhill hike lasting a total of six to seven hours can be interrupted after two hours in Kinídaros – or alternatively begun there. Around midday there is a bus connection – but enquire about times beforehand! Sights include the largest marble quarries on Náxos and later an unspoilt green valley with the ruins of a solitary church. Roads are used twice, otherwise the trail follows country lanes and paths through unspoilt landscape in the interior of the island. The kafenía in Kinídaros provide a good place to rest.
■ *15 km, difference in altitude 615 m, moderate to difficult*

AWT 0.00	After just over an hour our bus reaches **Stavrós-Keramotí chapel** (**P1**: N 37°06.362'/ E25°31.512', 650 m, see p.99 ①), which stands alone in a saddle between Apíranthos and Kóronos. This is a request stop. Take the road running
0.10	*downhill* exactly opposite the entrance. In the **second sharp right-hand bend** go left into a roadway, which soon crosses a small bridge. On the right lies the valley of
0.20	Keramotí. Having reached the shabby houses in **Kadís** ①, you find a marble table and a water tap.

You saunter down the roadway between gardens and, after the bend, catch sight of the notched marble mountains ②. Otherwise the area does not have much to look at. Disregard two right branch-offs. At a fork, where you go right, the old kalderími is visible under the roadway. In front of you lies a wide valley basin; dropping down into

it, you soon come to the road. Here, on the right, is a
0.55 **marble factory**, where the blocks are sawn. The workers
are pleased to give hikers a glimpse of their work.

Proceed right – up the road, over the hill and down to
1.10 **Kinídaros**, which has a well and some kafenía, not to
mention the bus stop on the square with the war memorial (**P2:** N37°06.045'/ E25°28.740', 400 m). Walk up the
steps on the left of a café, go right after 20 m, then left up
to a concrete track. Follow it to the left and, on the same
level, out of the village. Later you pass another marble
quarry, about 800 m away up on the right.
1.25 Pay no heed to a branch-off in a **saddle** (**P3:** N37°06.414'/
E25°28.684'). Instead take the footpath to the right 50 m
before a refuse tip; although a short cut, this quickly re-
joins the roadway. Later you see the white Ayios Artémios
church with three naves in the
valley – our next goal . In the
same line of sight, lower down
and some distance away, you
discern a newly laid, grey paved
track.
1.35 Soon you arrive at its **junction
to the right** and descend into
the valley in serpentines – on
the paving stones, then on the
original path. After seven minutes though you land back on
the roadway. But after 20 m another path runs downhill somewhat *inconspicuously*, ending
above the steep embankment of

the roadway. Here you must go back 20 – 30 m and look for a gentler drop to the roadway through undergrowth. Walk 150 m down it until where a wide mule track on the right descends in to the green valley basin. This path leads to a fork, to which you will later return.

> **Short cut:** As the church is deserted, and sometimes closed too, it might be an idea to go left already here.

Otherwise you proceed right, past the water mill (right) and right before the stream, which you traverse on stepping stones (**P4:** N37°06.856'/ E25°28.525', 170 m). The path runs uphill to a roadway, which you follow to the right. At the end you pass through a gate on the right and

2.05 easily find the path leading through the grove to **Ayios Artémios church.**

> *The church with three naves from the 18th century is the largest outside the town. Inside are just three altarpieces and one unadorned iconostasis ④. The mighty walls are however very impressive. A monastery is said to have stood here once, a ruined chapel can still be found in the vicinity.*

We return the same way: first along the country lane, then down to the stream and up the far side, across the irrigation channel as far as the already familiar fork. Here you stalk straight ahead/right through the bushes on the same level. Later the mule track runs downhill and along the irrigation duct to a roadway, which you take up to the left for some metres. Below a house with an imposing

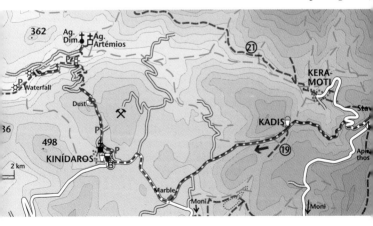

marble wall you meet the already familiar roadway and go to the right.

2.35 *Before* a large **bridge** you go right down to the stream, left underneath the first arch and on to the bank on the other side. There a veritable jungle path winds its way alongside

2.45 the stream. Crossing a **concrete weir** (**P5:** N37°06.632'/ E25°27.916'), you come to the left bank of the stream again and continue following the pretty trail through the wild valley ⑤.

Behind a fence you stumble across a roadway leading right, but leave it again at once by taking a footpath to the

3.15 right and passing **St. George's chapel** ⑥. Further down, after a house, you follow a roadway marked with wooden arrows. (If you fancy a dip, can go down an aqueduct beside this house and, in spring, discover a little pool further downstream – the turtles already know it.)

The roadway is lined with reeds on the left and comes to another track near a few houses. Leaving the valley, you

3.25 reach an **elevation**, which reveals a view of the fertile coastal plain of Engarés. On the right below our trail stands the uninhabited Venetian Pýrgos Brandoúna. High above it, directly below the summit in the north, is the legendary cave where Diónysos was born, today the white Jénnissis chapel.

At the first fork in **Engarés** (55 m) you stroll left between

3.40 the houses to the **road.** The bus only runs at the most unsuitable times. But since the coast road has quite a lot of traffic, it is possible to stop a car or hail a taxi. The place has two small inns to offer.

㉑ All alone on Náxos

This is the right trip for those who do not want to see any people for seven hours and who do not need kafenía or monasteries today. Path-finding skills are however a prerequisite. This very lovely hike mainly follows mule tracks, albeit difficult to make out in one section. The initially fertile, later more barren landscape possesses a good spring.
While it is possible to reach the starting point by bus, it is necessary to order a taxi on the way back (15 km). Maybe a nice driver will stop.

■ *12 km, difference in altitude 620 m, moderate to difficult*

AWT
0.00

Five kilometres beyond Apíranthos the **Stavrós-Keramotí chapel** ① stands alone on the road (650 m). This is where you alight and follow the vanishing bus another 30 m. At the end of the concrete retaining wall (left) you go down left and immediately through a gate. At the beginning the path is rather full of small stones, but later easier

0.10

to walk on, before it finishes at the **road.** Go down it for four minutes as far as a house (right), where you find the continuation of the path down on the left ②. It ends down at the car park in **Keramotí.**

0.20

Beyond the **church** (475 m) you go right and come to the concrete steps beside a gully running out of the valley. Ignoring a left-turn, you arrive at a

0.25

bridge in the shady valley (**P1**: N37°06.609'/ E25° 30.830'). Ascending out of the valley ③, you go straight ahead on the same level at a fork. A delightful path leads you along the hillside. Be sure to take in the view back towards Keramotí!

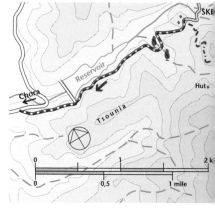

0.40 A little stone **bridge** (**P2**: N37°06.864'/ E25°30.377'), a
0.50 walled garden (left) and later a **goat-pen** (left) lie along
the way before you reach the plane trees standing in a dip
below a spring (**P3**: N37°07.075'/ E25°30.023', 410 m).
A romantic spot to rest – from here on it is more difficult
to locate the path. First you climb a bit and saunter along
more or less constantly at an altitude of 500 m ④. Down
in the valley on the left you see the Ayios Artémios
church with three naves concealed between trees ⑳.

1.45 **Two prominent rocks** ⑤ (**P4**: N37°07.385'/ E25°28.997',
530 m) narrow the path, before it runs across an elevation
and then downhill. Later there is a ditch down on the left.

2.20 Soon you **catch sight of** the reservoir down to the far left.
Orientation is difficult in this section, but even without a
path you manage to proceed through knee-high phrý-

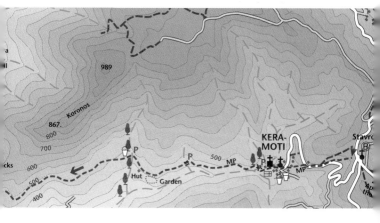

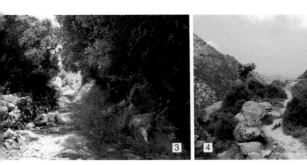

gana. About 300 m above a stone hut the mule track
2.30 swings right in to a wide hollow with an enormous **boulder** (right) (**P5:** N37°07.926'/ E25°29.387'). From here you climb again a little into a saddle with a high stone wall 50 m to the right. (Hidden behind this is the Ayía Sortíra chapel.)

Having walked round the hill on the right-hand side, you
2.40 **see** the few houses in Skepóni. Here you should keep to the right and look for an opening in the rock barrier, behind which the path can be clearly identified again.

3.00 Shortly before **Skepóni** you pass through a wire mesh gate and walk left along the roadway. Proceeding through
3.10 a dip with **planes** beside the stream course and along the
3.35 reservoir ⑥, you arrive at the **coast road** (30 m). Now you only have to make a friendly face and jump into the first car that stops!

㉒ The forty in Skadó

The two-and-a-half-hour, very charming round trip leads along footpaths between gardens to the almost deserted village of Skadó. From there it continues up across pasture land and along an old rock path back to Kóronos. Skadó has wells and a kind of taverna.

■ *5 km, difference in altitude 190 m, moderate*

AWT 0.00	From the **bus stop in Kóronos** you go past the memorial (p.106) and downhill for two minutes. At the car park you follow the sign "Iatreio" down the steps on the left. At the turn-off (town hall on the right) you walk straight ahead
0.05	on the same level to a **well** outside the town on the left (**P1: N37°07.190'/ E25°32.040'**). There you go 100 m up the concrete track, right at the top and steeply down the steps between vines. Up on the opposite slope lies our destination Skadó ①. After two minutes you reach a path running at right angles and turn left into it. This is the yellow marked long-distance trail N1 to Apóllonas.
0.15	In the hollow you traverse a watercourse near a **pump station** and then pant up the opposite slope. After six minutes you turn off up to the left and concrete steps take you past the small St. George's church with marble iconostasis.
0.25	Shortly afterwards you cross the **road** and climb between the houses in **Skadó**.

> *The village is almost deserted, 40 inhabitants are said to still live here. Sometimes noises can be heard behind the doors. The many ruins bear testimony to better times, when the menfolk found work in the emery mines.*

Where the stepped road forks, you enter the left alley and ascend left until you see a large church with a red tiled roof outside the village. However at the giant plane, 100 m before this church, countless concrete steps draw us up right to a water reservoir ②. Behind that we go right and up steps beside a concrete duct. This brings us to patches

0.35 with a five metre long **water basin.** We turn right there and walk along the right side of the basin on the same level for some metres and then uphill again beside a duct.

!! Two minutes later we *leave the duct* at a fork (**P2:** N37°07.615'/ E25°32.064') and ascend *right* on an initially gravelly path abundantly covered with vegetation. It

0.45 later becomes a real monopáti, which joins a **country lane** near a dilapidated shed and a wayside altar (left). Later going left along this, you wind your way up and get a wonderful view of Kóronos and the quarries above it, where emery is only sporadically mined nowadays (see p. 103).

0.55 The roadway **forks** indistinctly ③ (P3: N37° 07.598'/ E25°
!! 31.723'). Take a few paces horizontally to the left until you discover the wall that accompanies a monopáti. It runs down left, makes a right-hand bend and then runs along the hillside ④. Beautiful steps bring you safely back

1.25 down to **Kóronos.**

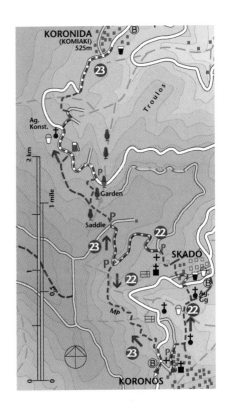

Emery mining in Kóronos

Emery was mined near Kóronos for more than 2,000 years. It is a mineral conglomerate consisting of corundum, magnetite, haematite and quartz which is almost as hard as diamond and is used as an abrasive.

The Kóronos mines flourished economically in the 1920s. Mining was stopped around 1990, as emery nowadays is almost entirely manufactured synthetically. Today the mines are only worked for two months a year in order to finance the miners' insurance.

An extensive network of pits still exists, parts of which can be visited. Also still standing are the pylons of the supply cableway which runs down to the port of transhipment, Moutsoúna. To commemorate this period, work has begun on the construction of a technical open-air museum, an older museum can be found on the road to Liónas.

㉓ Best on 21st May

The two-and-a-half hour hike along paths, briefly on lanes and a road too, runs across a mountain ridge from Kóronos to Koronída. The region is mostly used for agriculture, so it is also possible to find a well. The bus timetable allows almost five hours, which gives us time to discover Kóronos and its mining museum as well.

■ *6 km, difference in altitude 120 m, moderate*

▷ *Map see previous page*

AWT	In **Kóronos** you have time to amble through the steep alleys a little, before setting off along the road towards
0.00	Apóllonas at the **bust of Mandiláras** (p.106). After 150 m,
0.02	beyond the first left-hand bend, the **concrete track** branches sharply up to the left. After a short while it turns into to a marvellous monopáti ①, from which you later
0.10	**look down** on the cemetery. Then it runs on the right side of a high wall along the mountainside until coming
0.25	to a gorge. Rising up on the right are **high cliffs**, and
0.30	soon after the path joins a **country lane** (**P1:** N37°07.598′/ E25°31.723′).
0.35	This now leads you uphill rather steeply into a **saddle** (**P2:** N37°07.792′/ E25°31.736′, 790 m). In the direction you have come you discover a narrow path ② – more a gully in fact – and descend, eyes fixed on your destination Koronída. The path soon merges with a wider, still gravelly track, where you go left. After eight minutes you arrive at a water basin in the shade of plane trees.

	A distinct path leads you fairly directly into the valley and ends above a vegetable plot. Stepping stones jut out of the wall, then you find steps. 20 m above the road you walk
0.50	right for a bit through the **garden** and soon come across the last steps down to the road as well (**P3:** N37°07.972'/ E25°31.673') (The trail marked in the Anavasi island map is hard to find.)
1.00	Walk left, past the petrol station, to **Ayios Konstantínos chapel** with shady terrace beneath planes. If you come past on 21st May, you will leave it – sated and slightly tipsy – by the door on the other side. For panigíri, the consecration of the church, is celebrated here on St. Constantine's Day (see below). The rest of the year the well has to do instead.
	Below the chapel a lane descends on the other side of the road. It forks, we try our luck by going left, and again after
!!	20 m and are in luck: a barely perceptible *trail* runs
1.05	through the **dip** (580 m) and up to the road which leads
1.10	to **Koronída**. At the bus stop is an inn which serves strong coffee (see above).

Feast-Days – Panigíri

Often the hiker is fortunate enough to land completely unexpectedly in the middle of a religious festival. The church or chapel is bedecked with flags, a large congregation of guests in festive dress is sitting around – in their midst at least one priest. The tables are groaning under the weight of the food which the womanfolk or the owner of a private chapel have brought with them. Homemade drinks are proffered; canned drinks are sold at cost price. Immediately the stranger is invited to taste the many dishes and is involved in a conversation. These are unforgettable Greek moments.

The festivals take place on the name day of the patron saint of the church involved:

23rd April	Agíos Geórgios	20th July	Profítis Ilías
5th May	Agía Iríni	26th July	Agía Paraskeví
21st May	Agíos Konstantínos	27th July	Agios Panteleímon
Ascension Day	Agía Análipsi	6th August	Metamórphosis
Whitsuntide	Agía Triáda	15th August	Assumption Day
24th June	Ag. Ioánnis Pródomos	29th August	Agios Ioánnis
29th June	Agii Apóstoli	1st Sept.	Agios Mámas
7th July	Agía Kyriakí	14th Sept.	Stavrós

㉔ In Liónas valley

*Surely one of the most beautiful hikes on Náxos:
In three-and-a-half to four hours almost entirely on
paths through charming landscapes. Some inns,
but unfortunately no reliable wells. It is necessary
to organise the return journey from Liónas up to
Kóronos.*

■ *7 km, difference in altitude 560 m, moderate*

AWT
0.00
From the **bus stop in Kóronos** (with marble bust) you descend 200 m to the car park and on down Mandiláras alley on the far side. It is named after the man whose bust
stands further up. He was murdered at the time of the military junta.

Walk on down past the church (left), later right and uphill
slightly to the plátsa, which has two inns next to the covered well. With the well behind you, you walk back to the
left (not towards the inn "Bridge") and downhill until
you cross a small bridge after 200 m. Then you proceed
uphill slightly, right in front of a building with an outside
staircase and after 15 m go left. Soon you reach a concrete

0.10
path and stroll along, envied by others, ⬚, beneath trees.

0.15
Later, on the wayside, is a terraced **garden** (left), where
vehicle tracks begin. 80 m beyond the garden you leave

!!
these *by going left* into a path (**P1:** N37°07.216′/
E25°32.516′). It leads us into the green valley and down
right at a fork. Soon you traverse a small stone bridge and

★
amble on in the shade of planes. The water of the pretty
looking stream is unfortunately polluted by the village.

The trail broadens, it is possible to see further into the dis-

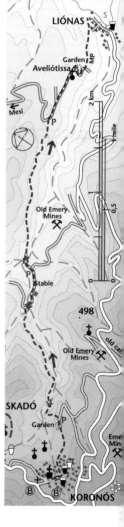

0.35 tance ②. Later you trek left above the green valley. Go through a **gate**, then in front of a wall down right to a

0.45 **stone bridge** ③ and a roadway.

Having walked 200 m up this, you traverse a closed-off goat pen. Five minutes later you turn off sharply down to the left (**P2:** N 37°07.877'/E

0.55 25°33.372') and then reach a **concrete bridge.** After three minutes the roadway ends at a gate. Now you go up left through the rocks to a monopáti, which climbs steeply.

At the top, from a height of 250 m, you have a splendid view across the valley; on the opposite side you can make out mineshafts. Emery has been mined here since Antiquity; it is used for grinding. 20 years ago the mines were almost closed, as industrially manufactured emery is cheaper. The remains of the supply cableway can still be seen against the rocks where an industrial monument is going to be installed.

A short section of the trail is overgrown and you have to make sure

!! you find it again *after 20 m* and do not drift off up to the left. At an altitude of about 200 m you walk towards the sea ④, until you meet the

1.30 **concrete track** which comes down from Mési (**P3:** N 37°08.241'/E 25°34.352'). Here you go down to the right, and again at the fork after

1.35 three minutes. A little later **Panagía Afdeliótissa chapel** lies just below the roadway, the entrance is a few metres further on.

After 200 m the track makes two serpentines and ends –

!! but not for us. Exactly where it ends, *beneath the garden wall,* is a trail which leads to a rough roadway. 50 m be-

1.45 yond the right-hand bend, on the left, begins a **path,**

which brings us without much fuss to the pebble beach of
1.55 **Liónas.** A lot has happened here in the last few years –
holiday houses, inns and hire cars: One of the latter may
give us lift back. Or, after a meal, you could ask the land-
lord to ring a local taxi under the no. 22850-24331. It
should however be up on the road shortly after 4 pm,
when the bus from Apóllonas drives past.

Sea connections to Náxos

Ships bound for the eastern Cyclades depart from two mainland
ports. The large ferry-boats sail from the main Athens port of
Piraeus to Santoríni, Rhodes and Sámos. They have stopovers at
Sýros, Mýkonos, Páros and Náxos. This connection takes five to six
hours as far as Náxos and is the more pleasant, and also cheaper,
alternative. As the daily departure is between seven and eight in
the morning, it may be wiser to stay overnight in Piraeus.
The second possibility is to sail from the small port of **Rafína**,
which is well served by buses from Athens airport. Departing from
there are faster, smaller ships which serve the northern Cyclades
with Mýconos and reach Náxos in four hours.
The connection from the charter airports Santoríni and Mýkonos
is irregular. In summer small excursion boats travel from Náxos to
Santoríni in the morning as an additional airport transfer.
Information on sea connections may be found in advance on the
internet at www.gtpnet.com or, at Athens airport, from the Greek
National Tourism Organization.

㉕ The unfinished god

After a dramatic bus journey through the mountains of Náxos you wander along a gently downhill incline to the huge, unfinished monumental statue of Apóllonas. The bus timetable allows four and a half hours for the tour. Tavernas are available at the beginning and end of the hike.

■ *7 km, difference in altitude 525 m, easy to moderate*

AWT
0.00

You take the first bus to **Koronída** (or Komiakí) (525 m). Unless you are in the mood to celebrate the exciting journey on the terrace of the local kafeníon, head down the

0.03

village street. At the *second* **sign** to the Mycenean grave (beside a concrete ramp) turn left up steps between high walls. After 50 m turn right at a steel railing and immediately left up the hill, until the path divides in front of a **group of houses**.

0.05

*Alternative: Proceeding straight ahead uphill, you reach the **Mycenean burial chamber** from the 15th century BC in three minutes. The hive-like structure measuring 3.5 m in width was erected for a chieftain and is one of the best-preserved graves on the Cyclades.*

The trail to the sea leads right horizontally from the above mentioned group of houses, then down between garden walls. Later you see a large war memorial on the right. Then the trail forks – you continue left, climbing slightly. This very beautiful trail up the slope ① affords a view of Donoússa on the right.

0.25
0.40

Disregard a **well-beaten track** to the left (**P1**: N 37°09.148'/ E 25°32.355', 385 m). After a bend you pass a **stable** on

the left, later walking directly
0.50 behind a **farm** (house 304) towards the sea. At a fork above
a house, go right through a
gate. Then left down to the
street and up it to the right as
far as the next right-hand
bend.

At the sign "Cul-de-sac" a **con-**
1.05 **crete track** runs left down into a shady, green valley with a
bridge and then up again to
1.15 the **road**, which runs slightly
downhill. Six minutes after
1.25 the **fork**, where you have gone
left, the sign "Koúros" guides
you left to the steps which lead
to the more than 10 metre
1.35 high monumental **marble**
statue ②.

> *On account of the beard it is
> assumed to be a statue of
> Dionysos. Hence it is no
> "koúros", no youth, but a
> god.*
> *Due to several material de-
> fects the statue was never
> completed. The poor god has
> therefore been lying in an
> uncomfortable oblique posi-
> tion in a former quarry for
> 2,500 years.*

Diagonally opposite, on the
other side of the road, you de-
1.40 scend to **Apóllonas**. Here you
run into large crowds of
tourists who have come by bus
for a quick meal in one of the
special restaurants set up to
cater for them.

Some Greek words for hikers:

Stress on the accents.

jássas	hello	kerós	**weather**
ne	yes	aéras	wind
óchi	no	meltémi	strong north wind
parakaló	please	ílios	sun
efcharistó	thank you	wrochí	rain
endáxi	okay	omíchli	fog
sto kaló	all the best		
kalá	lovely	níssos	**island**
símera	today	farángi, langádi	ravine, gorge
ávrio	tomorrow	kámpos, pláka	plains
pósin óra?	How long?	livádi	meadow
pósso makriá ine ja?	How far is it to...?	déndro	tree
		léfkes	poplars
puíne...?	Where is...?	dássos	forest
óra	hour	lófos	hill
neró	water	wounó, óros	mountain
psomí	bread	vígla	mountain peak
tirí	cheese	vráches	rock, cliff
míkro	small	spíleo	cave
mégalo	big	thálassa	sea
leoforió	bus	órmos	bay
stásis	bus stop	límni	lake
enikáso	rent	potámi	river
aftókinito	auto	réma	dry bed
mechanáki	motor bike	pigí	spring
podílato	bicycle	pérazma	pass, ridge
kaíki	boat	xirolithía	dry wall

hora	**city**	odiporió	**wandering**
horio	hamlet	isía	straight on
spíti	house	dexiá	right
platía	square	aristerá	left
parélia	harbour promenade	apáno	uphill
kástro	Venetian castle	káto	downhill
pírgos	fortified Venetian castle	kondá	near
		makriá	far
nekrotafío	cemetery	ásfalto	asphalt street
limáni	harbour	drómos	street
vrísi	fountain	chomaódromos	gravel street
stérna	cistern	dasikí odós	forest path
kafenío	café, and how!	odós	path
		skála	path of steps
eklisiá	**church**	monopáti	mule track
papás	priest	kalderími	paved way
moní, monastíri	monastery	katsikó drómos	goat path
ksoklísi	chapel	yéfira	bridge
panagía	Mother of God	stavrodrómi	crossing, intersection
panigíri	parish fair		
ágios, agía, AG	saint	hártis	map
ikonostasio	icon altar screen	kutrúmbulo	path marking
katholikón	central building in a monastery	phrýgana	scrub, the island hiker's enemy

Abbreviations, Key

▬▬▬	hiking route on a road or dirt track
▬▬▬	hiking route on a street
- - - - ·	hiking route on a path
··············	hiking route without a path
....ALT...ᴏᴏᴏᴏᴏ	alternative route, short-cut
← ⇐	walking direction / alternative
P	GPS point
═══	street
▬▬▬	dirt track, sandy track
MP ▣	monopáti, mule track / marking
— — —	dry stream-bed (at times), hollow
⚑	antenna
Ⓑ ⦙B⦙	bus stop / seasonal
ℙ	parking area
Ⓗ	helicopter landing pad
⊞	cemetery
+	wayside shrine, monument
⬭	sports field
⌒	cave
♪ ♂	medieval castle, dwelling tower / ruins
⛫	ancient ruins, statue
▪ ▫	houses / ruins
♦ ♦	monastery, large church / ruins
♦ ♦ ♦	chapel / summit chapel / ruins
▼ ⊟	taverna / open seasonally
✹ ☿	windmill/watermill, ruins
⌾ ▫ ▫	fountain, well, spring, reservoir, cistern
ꜱ	swimming possible

In the text:

!!	pay attention to turn-off!
↙	possible feelings of vertigo
OW	time for walking one way
★	the author's 10 favourite spots